POETOPIA

SUSSEX

Edited by Sarah Washer

First published in Great Britain in 2015 by:

Remus House
Coltsfoot Drive
Peterborough
PE2 9BF
Telephone: 01733 890066
Website: www.youngwriters.co.uk

Book Design by **ASHLEY JANSON**

SB ISBN 978-1-78443-829-6

Printed and bound in the UK by BookPrintingUK
Website: www.bookprintinguk.com

FOREWORD

Welcome, Reader!

For Young Writers' latest competition, Poetopia, we gave secondary school pupils nationwide the challenge of writing a poem based on the rules of one of 5 factions: Castitas for reflective, honest poetry; Temperantia for angry, assertive poetry; Humilitas for positive, uplifting poetry; Benevolentia for emotional poetry; and Industria for diligent, structured poetry. Poets who wrote a poem outside of these parameters were assigned to Dissimilis.

We chose poems for publication based on style, expression, imagination and technical skill. The result is this entertaining collection full of diverse and imaginative poetry, which is also a delightful keepsake to look back on in years to come.

Here at Young Writers our aim is to encourage creativity in the next generation and to inspire a love of the written word, so it's great to get such an amazing response, with some absolutely fantastic poems. Once all the books in the series are published we will pick the best poem from each faction to win a prize.

I'd like to congratulate all the young poets in **Poetopia - Sussex** - I hope this inspires them to continue with their creative writing. And who knows, maybe we'll be seeing their names on the best seller lists in the future...

Jenni Bannister

Jenni Bannister
Editorial Manager

THE FACTIONS

CASTITAS (Kas-ti-tas)

- Write a soul-baring, honest poem
- Tell us what it is like to be you
- Channel your confusion and emotions at being a teenager into verse

TEMPERANTIA (Temper-ran-tee-ah)

- Stand up for someone or something
- Vent your anger through poetry
- Express your frustration about a situation that's out of your control

HUMILITAS (Hu-mil-lih-tahs)

- Write a positive, uplifting poem
- Write an ode to celebrate someone or something that you appreciate
- Write a spiritual poem

BENEVOLENTIA (Ben-e-vol-en-tee-ah)

- Write a love / emotional poem
- Empathise with another's situation or predicament
- Write a praise poem
- Write a poem about your best friend / your friendship

INDUSTRIA (In-dust-ree-ah)

- Write a poem about current affairs
- Use a strict poetic form, such as a sonnet or kyrielle
- Research a poet of your choice and write in a similar style

DISSIMĬLIS (Diss-i-mĭl-is)

- If pupils write a poem that falls outside of the factions' rules, they become Dissimĭlis
- Poems can be on any theme or style

CONTENTS

THE POEMS

Brian Lion

I have not cried but just died
Ready for the ride
Heaven's doors slide
In I go
Very slow
God shouts
Brian the lion
Angels shout
Brian the lion
We dance
In the sun
When our jobs are done
Play for money
My nose is runny
God diminished bright light
Eat my meat, can't be beat
Dancing and playing
Take my seat
Can't be beat
Playing and dancing
All day
Until May
Well that's what I say
Time to eat my feast
I'm the beast
Taste my defeat
I can't be beat.

Bradly Sibanda (11)
Ark William Parker Academy, Hastings

I'm Flying

I'm fed up with life
I don't need a knife
I go up to a rock
I run and then I drop
As I plummet
I speed up to the limit
I remember life
Birth, childhood, hate . . .
As my eyes close, my mouth grimaces
Then silence . . .
But I don't die!
As my eyes open, I see clouds
I don't have pressure on my back
I look side to side – white wings!
I cross my eyes – an orange beak!
I scream but a screech comes out
The truth sinks in
I'm flying!

William Cramp (12)
Ark William Parker Academy, Hastings

Dreams

Hold fast to your dreams
Or they will deflate like melting ice cream
Dreams can escape through the gate
Light beams
Still no hope
Hold fast to your dreams
And everything will be OK.

Morgan Hay (12)
Ark William Parker Academy, Hastings

Love And Hate

The clock goes round, *tick, tick, tick*
Thunder clashing and banging, *clash, bang, clash*
Fun times, bad times
People dying, people laughing
Like when 9/11 happened, a sad moment in life
But a happy moment is when family join together
Like two peas in a pod
The world goes round day and night
Every hour, every night and day
Like a ball constantly spinning
Expressing anger isn't a bad thing
Like Batman expressing his anger at the Joker.

Reece Freeman (12)
Ark William Parker Academy, Hastings

Untitled

I brushed it away
As it has now gone
It streamed down
As it has been so long
My heart could not be fixed

You have done your deed
You can't help me now
But that's all I need
It's hurt me enough
But you don't care
And I suppose that's why we can't be a pair.

Freddie James Edwardes (12)
Ark William Parker Academy, Hastings

Living In Shame With Just A Fag To Your Name

Smoking kills you faster than choking
It's most common in Woking
I don't know how people are coping
It's like death from a packet
Which is rather dramatic
A drug that's spreading across the nation
Which makes us near extinction
That nicotine is killing faster than you can say winning
Kills mums and dad all over the world
So no one is safe
Now ditch the fag and go for a date
Fags are a waste of time
So if you're thinking about having a fag, don't do it
We don't want to lose another innocent citizen of our loving world.

Arian Ziarati (12)
Ark William Parker Academy, Hastings

Match Day!

6am in the morning, I wish I could sleep
But my alarm clock has spoke, 'Beep, beep, beep.'
Today is the match
A momentous day
Maybe the keeper can't catch
Maybe it will go your way
But you came here to play
Now it shall be your day
So make it go your way
You're a star
Meanwhile your coach is relaxing at the bar
You are getting ready in your red and blue car
You can make this day go your way!

Harvey Wickison (12)
Ark William Parker Academy, Hastings

Ghost

As quick as a flash
I saw a ghost
I gazed in fear
But on I went
I saw glossy blood
Along the treen

How could I go on?
Bang, bang
I heard a gunshot
The wind whistled
Thunder struck . . .

Liam Thurston (12)
Ark William Parker Academy, Hastings

Irongate

Listen up maggots, you're in my prison now escaping, huh!
Don't make me laugh
Our prison guards gonna break you in half
Porridge for meals, I'm not making any deals
You want to mess with our stuff, don't be daft
We got tasers, your weapon's a mop
Hope you're not squeamish, because if so you'll drop
You play by my rules, now eat up your gruel
Using a vent, may as well put up a tent
You had a family, hope you said bye
Cause you mess with me, you're gonna die.

Seth Brookes (12)
Ark William Parker Academy, Hastings

Summer Day Surprise

6am in the morning, not a noise was heard as I was snoring.
But my alarm clock begged to differ, as it's time lied, making it go *beep! Beep! Beep!*
As I woke up I was met with a dull surprise, we had to go shopping bucket loads
When we drove off we passed loads of shops, not one did we stop.
I asked my mum where we had gone, she smiled at me and told me to look at the sign
Legoland!
All the seemingly hours which weren't long at all were all worth it,
To see the entrance of Legoland clear like water!

Adam Cachrimanis (11)
Ark William Parker Academy, Hastings

Factionless

Rushing through my veins, taking over my blood stream
Boom, boom! My heart, gradually beating, faster, faster!
Flooding through me, I feel: hate, diligence, honesty.
Anger, burning
Being fuelled by my never-ending rage,
It was as though a raging rhino was trapped inside of me
Drip, drip! The endless dripping of blood,
Infuriating me even more, a fire burning inside of my heart
Emerging through all of my anger, is hope calming the storm
I am the odd one out of the pack
I am Dissimilis.

Sam Tomlin (12)
Ark William Parker Academy, Hastings

Skating

Skating
It's so fun
You can ride on two or four wheels
And go fast down hills

When you're on ramps
You may fall off and get hurt
And have blood on your shirt
But you can get up and skate again

Once you're good you can do tricks and flicks
And it's so fun.

Josh Mann (12)
Ark William Parker Academy, Hastings

Kick Racism Out!

Racism is bad
It makes me mad
You must be insane
To call someone a name
Because of their religion
Colour or creed
Come on people, there is just no need
We were put on this planet to be treated the same
Come on everybody let's play a fair game
Kick racism out!

Kian Epps (12)
Ark William Parker Academy, Hastings

First Badminton Match

My first match, I hope I win
The shuttle drops as I serve
Hoping I can win my first point
My first match
The day to show, what I can do
This is my day
Hoping it will go my way
I win the point, that I will remember for all my life
The game is over
I win my first ever badminton match.

Ryan Burdett (12)
Ark William Parker Academy, Hastings

My Painful Life!

Fights with my brother
My mom don't bother
Laying in bed
Whist holding my head
Getting up quick
Feeling a bit sick
Quiet as a mouse
I leave da house
Going to school
I feel like a fool.

Craig Brett (11)
Ark William Parker Academy, Hastings

Champions League

The Champions League Final
Who's going to win?
Juventus or Barcelona?
Drogba or Messi?
The stadium is going to be as shaky as a rocking boat
I can see in the people's eyes, thinking
Who's going to win that big shiny trophy
The people are shouting at each other
Like World War III was about to begin . . .
I wish I could be there one day.

Wills Brown (12)
Ark William Parker Academy, Hastings

Nepal Earthquake

In Nepal people die
As the terror goes on
The ground rumbles
As the ground crumbles
Thousands of people have died
They fall like dominoes in the breeze
Homes wrecked that look like bricks
Have been thrown at them
Their lives end in seconds
Nature is more powerful than people.

David Towner (12)
Ark William Parker Academy, Hastings

Christmas Time

A time of joy and laughter
Helping the poor and opening presents
Full of excitement
The happiest time of the year

The cheers of putting up the tree
And hanging up the sparkling decorations of Christmas

Christmas is the diamond of the year
Always shining bright like a star in the sky
Giving hope and joy to all.

Jonathon Beaton (11)
Ark William Parker Academy, Hastings

The Pitch Of Joy

The pitch of joy
Is where we always are
Never to be beat
The best players ever

We strive to achieve
And become the best we can
The golden ball so light and bright
As we kick it to the back of the goal!

Mikkel Fisher (12)
Ark William Parker Academy, Hastings

Rage In My Blood

R eally
A ngry
G etting
E nraged

I 'm
N ever on

M y own
Y oghurt tries to calm me

B eing
L oved
O n someone's side
O nly being
D epressed over not helping is worse.

Matthew Potter (12)
Ark William Parker Academy, Hastings

My Christmas

Each year more exciting
The 25th of December
Even as a small child
It was something I would remember

The countdown till Christmas
Putting up the bright lights
Getting a fantastic Christmas tree
Much larger than my height

Cold winter mornings
A fire giving a warm glow
Wrapping up all the presents
And adding a decorative bow

At last it is the eve
When Santa and Rudolph come
I jump into a cosy bed
Dreaming of Christmas pud in my tum

'Tis the morning full of joy
I cry, 'It is finally here,'
We walk down the stairs together
Into the room full of Christmas cheer.

Megan Geall (15)
Chichester High School for Girls, Chichester

The Photo

I look at the frame upon the shelf
The one that encloses a picture of myself
It makes me remember that specific night
Sitting at a table with a candle light

The frame is the one I bought that day
With only three euros I had to pay
It makes me remember that specific night
When the food was perfect with every bite

I am wearing my beautiful red dress
It is my favourite I must confess
It makes me remember that specific night
When I was drinking that ice-cold Sprite

My hair is down, my shades are on
Even though the sun is gone
It makes me remember that specific night
Caught up in a Cyprus twilight

The photo is a momento of my holiday
The one I spent with my family
It makes me remember that specific night
Along with the previous fortnight.

Chloe Smith (15)
Chichester High School for Girls, Chichester

Modern Life

15 years ago, I was born in September,
this was a great day, that I do not remember.

A baby I was with no care in the world,
I grew my first teeth and my hair was all curled.

15 years later, I live by the sea,
a teenager doing a GCSE.

Unwillingly forced to do work every day,
when really I want to go out or just stay

At home, like the days when I was small, only five.
Those were the days when I really did thrive.

But now I am stuck in a building to 'learn'.
To travel, explore, that's what I do yearn.

Getting qualifications, those As, those Bs,
this is the issue that nobody sees.

These letters do not represent who you are,
without them you could still get just as far.

Ashia Sadler (15)
Chichester High School for Girls, Chichester

Love Poem

The melons you own
Are most definitely shown
The cackle in your voice
Only gives me one choice

Your figure adds up
I'm beginning to think I was love struck
Your tan is a tiramisu
Oh my word, just look at you

Your personality is perfect
If you leave me I'll object
I'll take you to court
Your sentence won't be short

Now you're imprisoned
Sorry, should've listened
Bye
Good
Thanks for listening.

Siede West (18)
Greenfields School, Forest Row

Valentina

Your eyes are chocolate
Your dimples adorable
Your chuckle like a chicken
You're always so joyful

Buying clothes in the mall
Joining in games of football
Conversations in the middle of the night
I can trust you with anything
My secrets, my regrets, my past

We share everything from clothing to treats
Being around you is always so sweet
Sometimes it feels like you stick to me like glue
But I still can't imagine a day without you.

Fatema Alhawaj (15)
Greenfields School, Forest Row

The Beach

The bright sun was shining
My brother was whining
There were people fishing
The sand was sizzling

You could smell the suntan lotion
We threw rocks into the ocean
The white cliffs were cracked
The fish were being attacked
Seagulls were squawking
People were walking

Children were building sandcastles
They opened their food parcel
We were splashing in the sea
I fell over and hurt my knee.

Joe Liggett (11)
Seahaven Academy, Newhaven

My Very Special Friend

Every day I live for you
To let the whole world know what you have done for me

The first day I met you
I completely fell in love with you
My life is easier
Because you are in it
Just to know you
Fills my heart with joy
I love you
Beyond words I can say

You are the reason
I haven't given up
You embrace me with your love
I can't imagine living without you
You complete me

You never forget me
You know my deepest needs
No matter what
You have my best interests at heart

It all started with a message
You spoke a thousand anthems into my ear
You are perfect in every way
When I look out to the sea
I think about the great love you have for me
You are completion
I need you in my life
I love you forever
My very special friend.

Claire Lucy Garman (15)
Seahaven Academy, Newhaven

My Angel

Once I saw an angel
And he smiled
When he smiled
Peace lilies tremored in the wind

Oceans drifted in euphoric doze
The sun smiled back at his angel
And he lit up the world's eyes

Soft wind blew
And pixies swam playfully
Through his beautiful hair
Pansies and tulips gazed at him
Through the tall grass

His eyes were pure
Oblivious to hate and fear
His voice
Each word he whispered
As a gentle lullaby
His spirit was twinned
With innocence

He looked at me for refuge
And I kept him
Safe through the years
They wouldn't have understood
Understood that he had to be kept pure

They'd lie, cheat
Steal and crush him
All the haters, doubters
Anger, revenge would

He'd start to lose hair
Beautiful hair
They'd starve him of hope
And faith and he'd
Fall gently to the ground
Still and silent

All the time they fall
To the ground

But not this one, he's mine
I wish I could save all the others
But I can save him
We'll play and dance
In the rain and sun
Growing and changing
Through the years
He'll stand tall for eternity.

Lulu Williams (15)
Seahaven Academy, Newhaven

Their Wrecked Story

Her life has not been great
Her father has never loved or liked
His drunkenness controlled his life
He abused her little brother
For almost half his life

He was never in the house
He was Satan's twin
For he looked back to see
His mistake
Crying herself to sleep, wanting a real dad
He would stay up
All night from 3am to 3pm
He always falls over

She saw him once on her own, she was scared
For he had become a monster for children
He never got help, she never stood up
But when her mum did, swearing began
It's not very fair waking up every day wishing to see him
When you only have pictures, he sends letters
Her dad's life, my life
He was only five and she was only seven
Now they are ten and twelve and happy without him
Knowing that he has gone.

Ria Stride (11)
Seahaven Academy, Newhaven

Bullying

Nobody likes a bully
And a bully likes no one
Least of all themselves

They pick and prod at their victims
'You're fat, ugly and dumb!'
But what do they see in the mirror
And do they hate what they have become?

We must stand up to the bullies
Stand up for ourselves and our friends
We must show we can overcome this
Then the bullying can finally end.

Alfie Webster (11)
Seahaven Academy, Newhaven

Best Friends

I've got a best friend
She's a wonderful girl
She's got nice brown hair that turns into curls
If I was hurt then she would be there
She would help me for always and be there to care
She keeps her cool when she's annoyed and angry
She ignored nasty comments as she walks about grandly
She likes to text me day and night
She's so clever she gets everything right
This poem is about you and I hope you like it
Because everything's true and I think you know it
You're always calm and at ease
Because the perfect girl is called Louise.

Maddi Davis (11)
Seahaven Academy, Newhaven

Friendship

This is one of life's greatest treasures
And something that needs to be measured
Best friends stick together until the end
They are like a straight line that never bends

Laughter and cheer from you to me
Two best friends are better than three
Best friends are there for you through good and bad
They are there to make you laugh when you are sad

Just because you don't see them every day
That doesn't mean their heart is in the wrong place

They are always there
And always care
Friends like that are very rare
You could be small you could be tall
Sizes and looks don't matter at all

A friend like you is one of my greatest treasures.

Shannon Marie Nairn (12)
Seahaven Academy, Newhaven

Love

When tough love brings you down
Try your hardest not to frown
Remember to keep trying
Stop all your crying
The feeling of love
When the good days come
And it's hard for some
Let them know
How to grow
The feeling of love.

Taylor Clark (12)
Seahaven Academy, Newhaven

Cancer

It's a word no one wants to hear
Normally it's crystal clear
You're here one minute but gone the next
You can have it whilst you text

Lots of people have to suffer
Even a child or its mother
Doctors say you need surgery
But even that might not set you free

This is what people dread
In an instant it can spread
You will release a tear
When you finally have a fear
Of this terrible thing so near
You might not even have a year

For Jackie.

Leianna Stamp (12)
Seahaven Academy, Newhaven

Leianna, My Star

F orever together
R espect for one another
I 'll be there for you
E specially when you're there for me
N o one can break our bond
D arkness can't outshine our light
S unlight shines on us
H elping each other through the rough times
I wouldn't know what I would do without you
P eople can make fun of us but they're jealous

L eianna, my best friend, my sister, my star
A lways by my side
S tanding tall together
T omorrow's just another day for us to show off our friendship
S tanding together until the end.

Jasmin Louise Huxtable-Strong (12)
Seahaven Academy, Newhaven

Frustration

Head spinning
Blood boiling
Pulse rising
Frustration
An outrage from within
Over an opponent's win
My head is in a spin

I can't see straight
No time to wait
Frustration
I nearly had a bite
But it put up a fight
And swam away in the night
Frustration

It kills me from inside
And I can't hide
Frustration.

Albi Paris (12)
Seahaven Academy, Newhaven

Daddy

My dad was laying
Then I was praying
If he will be fine
Stay alive

I was upset
When he slept
I give my luck
I love our pug
I love you Daddy

Stay strong
Don't do wrong
Love you lots Daddy.

Leo Houston (12)
Seahaven Academy, Newhaven

The Devil In I

A nger rushes through you like boiling water
N obody understands but they think they do
G ot to get out but the anger traps you
E ating you away, feasting on your fears
R aging, emotions all muddled up.

Hermione White
The St Leonards Academy, St Leonards-On-Sea

A Letter To Mum And Dad

'No,' they said
'You can't stay
Just leave
Just go away.'

They'd laugh at me
And push me down
I couldn't do anything
I was their clown.

They'd tease me
And pull my hair
And I tried to act
Like I didn't care.

I did care though
Deep down inside
They didn't know
How much I cried.

I told them to stop
But they said, 'No.'
And it carried on
And I sank low.

I wasn't worth it
I wasn't good enough
But in front of the world
I tried to act tough.

I started getting tired
Of everything really
But believe me when I say
I'll miss you clearly.

I hope you understand
I just couldn't do it anymore
Not with them here
Telling me I'm a bore.

An idiot
A waste of space
Worthless
Without a time or place.

Maybe it was me
Maybe I'm all wrong
Maybe I tried too hard
Maybe I've been here too long.

Mum and Dad
This wasn't you
It wasn't your fault
There was nothing you could do.

Even if they did stop
I'd remember forever
The way they said
I'd never be good enough, ever.

I couldn't escape them
Without leaving completely
But I didn't want everyone to know
So I'll do it discreetly.

I'm really sorry
I really am
But putting up with them?
I don't think I can.

Don't tell everyone
I don't want false sympathy
All I ask
Is that you remember me.

So be happy now
Please don't cry
I won't be in pain
After this goodbye.

Malana Lane Topham
The St Leonards Academy, St Leonards-On-Sea

At First His Love . . .

The love we all desire
Burns bright just like a fire
It blossoms like a flower
Impossible to overpower

It doesn't scream or cry in pain
And is not held back by a chain
She got the love she once desired
The one true love everyone would admire

Every day gave her a thrill
A new adventure to fulfil
In her eyes the love they shared
Unexpectedly followed by the pain she bared

His love for her changed like the seasons
Her sadness grew for the worst of reasons
She lay in bed unable to sleep
Because her thoughts were too deep

Her heart was broken into a million pieces
As his love for her quickly decreases
She wiped a tear from her eye
As he then turned into the bad guy

He once promised her every night
Before the darkness swallowed the light
Before the sun began to close
The crimson moon then slowly arose

He slowly swallowed up her pride
As the devil offered him a ride
He took the chance and left her broken
Ruining her by his words clearly spoken

Her dream was a dream until it came true
It turned into a nightmare she wished she never knew
A certain darkness is needed to see the stars
But this darkness left her soul in scars.

Sharana Agginie-Elliott (13)
The St Leonards Academy, St Leonards-On-Sea

Why Lie?

Why must you lie
To make me cry
And today I say
Goodbye.
You should ask yourself
Why lie,
To make us cry?
Drip
Drip
Drip
I am a small whimper
I am a small ant lost in a forest
I am a small raindrop dripping
Down a car window.
Drip
Drip
Drip
Do you like to cover your own back?
Or is it to not be a fool?
There's plenty of ways that resolve
The problem
Just don't lie
To make people cry.
I feel lonely
I feel sad
I feel miserable
I feel gloomy
Drip
Drip
Drip
How do you feel – sad, happy or angry?

Kurtis James Clark (12)
The St Leonards Academy, St Leonards-On-Sea

The Janoskians' Best Beautiful Boys Dance

Whispers going around the crowd
Soon the whispers stop
And turn into loud screams

They enter the stage
Big smiles on their faces
Fans scream
As loud as roaring tigers

Crash! Bang!
The drums begin
Best Beautiful Boys dance
Happily the Janoskians sing away

Mouth-watering, to die for, dreamily
They are so amazing, special, epic, adorable

Everyone is dancing rapidly
Best Beautiful Boys dance
Water splashing from their bottles

Lovestruck as they look dreamily into my eyes
Their dance moves make me fall to the floor
Best Beautiful Boys dance
My eyes pop out of my head seeing them

The music stops
The crowd goes wild
Leaving the stage
Fans scream

Best Beautiful Boys dance.

Shania Jane Jean Hollingworth (14)
The St Leonards Academy, St Leonards-On-Sea

Spring And Summer

Oh spring!
The promise of a new start
Fresh and awakening
Your golden leaves and your chirping birds
The smell of the flowers
As I soak up the sun
But your rain when not expected
Leaves me all glum.
Then summer comes along
The barbecues, the summer songs
The long, long holidays
Oh summer!
You make me as happy as a sunflower
How I love your sunlight at dusk and at dawn
Oh summer!
You make me smile
Like when I open my first Christmas present.
As much as the ice creams and the melting sun
I always look back on the time spent
When you're not around
I long for your return
Please don't go away
Oh summer and spring!
The long autumn walks
The happiness you bring
So till the next year you come around
I'll let you prepare for the next time
You light up the ground.

Beulah Griffiths (13)
The St Leonards Academy, St Leonards-On-Sea

The Fallen Soldiers

He was just an ordinary person
What did he do wrong, to end up here?
He just stood there while everyone took a shot at him
He couldn't take it anymore
He fought back
Who he thought were his allies
They didn't care
He was shot in the leg
Shot in the arm
But they did nothing

He woke up in a few days wondering where he was
Surrounded by strangers checking he was good
The curtains enclosing him with a drip in his arm
He heard them saying, 'He can go back at dawn'
Not again, I can't go back through hell, he thought
He had seen the devil
But they were the enemies
'Now I'm just hoping it ends soon,' he said

Back in this hole with my fallen friends
We were loyal to one another
But they have all gone
The cracking sounds of the bullets over me
Just pop my ear drums
The explosions surround me
But I finally wake
Back without my friends
In a better place.

James Laidlaw (13)
The St Leonards Academy, St Leonards-On-Sea

Hard At War

I hate the way war happened
It felt like you don't know what to do
I sat there with my friend talking like nothing was going to happen
The smell horribly invaded my nostrils
We heard lots of gunshots and they were all around us
The feeling of fright as we walked
Thinking we would get shot
As we saw bodies floating to the floor, as it got tense
As we steamed through, dodging the bullets
As we got closer we rapidly shot at the enemy, hoping they wouldn't shoot back
The sound of thunder as we got closer to victory
Suddenly, I got out of control thinking what might happen next
Fast, a bullet rushing past at me I just stood there
Then whilst it came towards me I was thinking
Why should I be here?
Unfortunately the bullet hit me
Lots of blood splurting out of me onto the floor
When I woke up I saw people around me
They were doctors
The doctors just stood there talking to me
They were saying, 'He got shot,' and the bullet's still in me
I woke up, made the doctors jump
Saying, 'I want this bullet out of me'
I just heard some good news
The war has stopped and Great Britain drove to victory.

Mason Harris (14)
The St Leonards Academy, St Leonards-On-Sea

Homework – Haiku

As I grow older
I get angry more often
Mostly with homework.

Caine Davey (12)
The St Leonards Academy, St Leonards-On-Sea

Addiction

Here we go
Turn on the console
Two days ago, started on gaming
Like I fell in a hole
Devastated, innovated, I won't stop
It's addictive, that's illustrated
I'm addicted

It's scary, I play 'Erie'
I'm like a scorpion
Like Kratos, I will avenge
I'm not Mario
Can't save myself

I'm as cold as sub-zero
I said I will become a hero
The emotions drive me crazy
Here we go peach and daisy

I'm bored, I need a new game
Dear Lord, I go Gamestop
I shall go aboard
I'm a assassin, the black flag is mine
No! I'm not bluffing
I'm as serious as a mage mysterious
No! I won't give up, I will be the best
No wonder I thought I was blessed.

Richard Silis (14)
The St Leonards Academy, St Leonards-On-Sea

Happiness

I am an ice cream dripping down the cone
I am a glimmering jewel hanging off a chain
I am a sunray skimming the stones
I am a freezing cold glass of water on a yellow summer's day.

Jodie Cruttwell (12)
The St Leonards Academy, St Leonards-On-Sea

Vacant Vacation

I avoid the shattered stones and battered bloody blades
My shoes crunch on sharp shells and tatty blackout shades
Clearly the leftovers of last night's teen beach bash,
Where murder spawned and friends were torn
With their own gutter cutters and trash.

I peek at the acid people and their flaccid weak limbs
And their coke-infused tears that fill this filth town to the brim
The semi-grey faces, and their wicked, wild looks that say
'Hey, I've got a stabber and it's comin' right at you!'

Then there's the leather cladded clan
Who glare in such disgust
At anyone who hasn't had an ASBO or been cuffed
And the shoe gazers who hide behind the 2p slot machines
Who sit, wonder, wait, and watch
For nothing more than glee.

Once again I sheepishly peer over
At the ice cream man who's apparently sober
And serving spit-gazed week old pavlova
To nuclear families with their quirks and Range Rovers,

What is this world I'm living in
It's supposed to be a beach
But nothing than sweat, grit and grime
Is what this town can preach.

Haydn Eliot Ackerley (15)
The St Leonards Academy, St Leonards-On-Sea

For All You've Done

We once got on
We laughed, we cried
Me and you together
We beat all weathers
We shared our secrets, we shared our thoughts
We were an army
Who never got caught
We were best friends
But now we're not
But at the end of the day, it's all your fault

I wish you could see
See what you've done
The tears I shed
The pain I overcome
You were all I had
The only one I trusted
When you left me
You left me alone
No one to turn to
No one to talk to
I had nothing
You had everything
I'll never forgive you
For all you've done.

Sommer Cook (14)
The St Leonards Academy, St Leonards-On-Sea

Overthinking

Sadness filling my body
Following me around like a stalker
On a dark night
I feel like I've been used
Never again
I'm coldhearted, I'm nothing
It never ends,
Never a new beginning
Smaller than a grain of sand
Is how I feel
Death lingers through my head
I never asked for this, so why me?
I hope he understands but he won't
He's a boy
What do they understand?
It follows me like a lost sheep
All day, every day
I didn't ask for this, so why me?
We were so close
Always together, never apart
Maybe it wasn't love
I didn't ask for this, so why me?
I miss him, I love him
But I didn't ask for this, so why me?

Jodie Pfundstein (13)
The St Leonards Academy, St Leonards-On-Sea

I Am . . .

I am the rain trickling on the rooftops
I am the wind howling down the trees
I am the thunderstorm crashing over the sky
I am a blizzard chilling down your bones
I am the snow freezing the rooftops.

George Smith (12)
The St Leonards Academy, St Leonards-On-Sea

My Day At The Beach

A sunburnt face
Sand between my toes
The saltwater splashes
All up my clothes
Hunting for seashells
And surfing the waves
Makes everything seem okay

Building a sandcastle
Fit for a king
Makes all of my dreams
Come out from within
Wearing my shades
And getting a tan
Makes everything seem okay

Going to the beach
Makes all my dreams reach
Ocean breeze blowing
Feet kick and splash
Ocean waves breaking
With an almighty crash
I stretch my arms out
As far as they'll reach
Makes everything seem okay with a day at the beach.

Emily Cruttenden (14)
The St Leonards Academy, St Leonards-On-Sea

Cold

I am the sun sparkling in your face
I am the rain pouring on the rooftop
I am the wind blowing around the trees
I am a thunderstorm crashing on the fence
I am a blizzard chilling down in your garden
I am the snow freezing in your face.

Megan Hagland (14)
The St Leonards Academy, St Leonards-On-Sea

Coward

Day after day this hellhole
Treats me with no respect
For evermore the pain will last
Never leaving me in peace

You ask for respect but
All you get is misery in return
By the end of the day it feels like you've just had enough
You want to kill yourself
Just to take away the pain
This hellhole that desires you
The demons want to pull you down
Nothing else to do so
Leave it at that

These desolate holes of despair
Scurrying with pain and your best friend
Dead beside you
The stars in the sky is all you remember
Before that final bullet . . .
That is it
You are done
Branded a coward and lost
Nothing else, *bang* goes the final shot.

Jordan Rayment (14)
The St Leonards Academy, St Leonards-On-Sea

Untitled

Oh I don't like you,
All you do is have a go,
But sometimes I hope you don't
When I see you,
I flipping hate you
Why do you hurt me all the time?
Goodbye, I'm leaving you.

Joshua Weightman
The St Leonards Academy, St Leonards-On-Sea

Bully, Bully, Bully

I really hate bullying
It really grinds my gears
I don't know why you do it
But I'm sure heaven knows
That you'll be the next devil bird.

Callum Grinham
The St Leonards Academy, St Leonards-On-Sea

Home

This is my place
This is where I feel safe
It is where I run around
Around and have a laugh
This is my place

This is my place
This is where I feel
Like a loose lace
It is where I'm free
This is my place

This is my place
This is where I can
Snuggle up in bed
Like a phone in a case
It is where I can sleep
This is my place

This is my place
This is where I can hug
My mum and embrace
It is where I have warmth
This is 'home'.

Ryan Kent (1212)
The St Leonards Academy, St Leonards-On-Sea

Hounds Of Hell

As the blood boils, the hounds of hell start to rise
As the guards of heaven stand strong
The fear flows through the veins

As the fires from hell burn in the dark
The anger rises with the temperature
The guards with their battens and shields stomp forwards ever so slightly
Stopping the hounds turning the goodness into darkness.

Matthew Hunt (13)
The St Leonards Academy, St Leonards-On-Sea

Natural Love

The grass is green, the sea is blue
Animals run around with no clue
What to do

The trees sway as the wind blows
Leaves fly, babies cry, mothers love as most mums do

Love is all around, hearts pound
Praises loud, nothing is better than a natural friendship.

Nicholas Duly (14)
The St Leonards Academy, St Leonards-On-Sea

Untitled

Imagine
Lost in darkness
Sad, alone
You feel like screaming
Crying is all you can hear
Who will be next in that exam room?
I wonder, have I done well enough?
Have you ever felt like you want to die
With the stress?
Exams
They want us to fail
Sadness and fear will fill you to the brim
No one knows what they do to you
Exams
Silence
It makes you feel uneasy
Then you give into the stress
Exams, exams, exams then fail
Fail
Exams, stress and then fail
All come with exams
Teenagers, we all feel sorry for you!

Chelsey Kelly (12)
The St Leonards Academy, St Leonards-On-Sea

I Wish You Could See

I wish you could see
See the tears I cry
With every sharpened knife
I fade for a while

I wish you could see
See the way I fought
For you were mine
And I was yours

I wish you could see
See the love I had for you
Slowly burning
And it's all because of you

I wish you could see
See that I feel alone
Memories in a box
Closed for a lifetime

I wish you could see
See how I no longer care
Oh it all starts again
With another friend.

Briony Rose (14)
The St Leonards Academy, St Leonards-On-Sea

Oh I Think You Are . . .

Oh I think you are as red as fire
You're my desire
You are brilliant and courageous
When you cheer I drink beer
You make me proud
I am a cloud
Your talent is good
I am meant to get food!

William Evans (13)
The St Leonards Academy, St Leonards-On-Sea

My Poem

There's something hiding underneath my bed
It's always bad thoughts in my head
Sometimes thinking can lead to dread
But there's something underneath my bed.

No it will not leave my head
Life is just full of dread
Be warned for I have said
There is something underneath . . . your bed!

Maximus Parsons (12)
The St Leonards Academy, St Leonards-On-Sea

The Execution Ground

Here lies the execution ground
The silence creeps in, no sound
The temper is being raised each second
No one knows what should be reckoned
Here lies the execution ground

Hate, hunt, hurt, hell
My fuming heart pounding
Like a lightning bolt, powering up
And ready to strike
This devil lies in the cell

The sea of flames arise from the dead
The cold flare lights the bed
Inhabitants circling the extinct
Creatures who lie at their feet, yet
Running away is their natural instinct

My blustery mind boiling over
I really wish that this was over
The circus is untouched
Ready for the strike out
Here lies the execution ground.

Saffron Mamujee (13)
The St Leonards Academy, St Leonards-On-Sea

The Big Race

I start my engine
Rev, rev out the pits
I say Brands Hatch is no match for me
Red
Yellow
Green
Go
And I'm out!
Someone has already spun out
I'm in second
And first place was getting faster
I'm catching up
I put it into 6th and I feel a bit of a wobble
It was nothing
I put my foot down
And then
Bang
I'm into the gravel
But suddenly
Bang
Nothing.

Billy Best (14)
The St Leonards Academy, St Leonards-On-Sea

Teddy The Puppy

My puppy is so cute
She is so soft
She bounces around
She barks at footballs

I walk her every day
She loves long grass
She loves cuddles
She's starting to act like my cat.

Jade Burt (14)
The St Leonards Academy, St Leonards-On-Sea

It

It is deadly
It can kill
If you see It
You shall say, 'Goodbye.'

It will shake the Earth
It can knock down buildings
It can take people out in one hit
So watch out,
For it is nature.

Reuben Benge (12)
The St Leonards Academy, St Leonards-On-Sea

Anger

I stand there not knowing what to do
Frustrated, it's hard to think
Trying to express my anger
But it never seems to take my mind off anything
I stand there not knowing what to do
I feel like I just want to let it all out
But no one wants to listen
All I want is to be happy
I want to live a good life
But I can't control my anger
I stand there not knowing what to do
Helplessly, trying to find a way to get the anger out, any way
But it's hard, not knowing how to
I stand there not knowing what to do
I lay there endlessly thinking what to do
But it never works, I've tried getting a hobby but it never works
I've tried talking to my parents, but I can't
I've tried talking to the school helpers but I don't know them
And I can't get the words out
I stand there not knowing what to do
With all the thoughts in my head.

James Hucker (14)
The St Leonards Academy, St Leonards-On-Sea

Sad

Sad is grey like a wrecking ball,
It tastes like rotting meat
It smells like something dying
It looks like snowy sleet
It sounds like crying people
It feels like damp, wet clothes
It surrounds you when you least expect
And makes your cold tears flow.

Dione March (13)
The St Leonards Academy, St Leonards-On-Sea

The Men Who Came

The people cried as they came
They came with death, they came with pain
And all we had worked through went down the drain

They brought deceit, they brought lies
They brought new creatures like bees and flies
But soon they too went down to Hell
Taking people as they fell

And soon we too go down that well
To go with Man, with Man from Hell.

Matthew Bothwell (13)
The St Leonards Academy, St Leonards-On-Sea

Hero Of War

Grabbing the wet ladder in the trench
He shakily raises his right leg
Looking straight forward into darkness
Listening for the order
Adrenaline rushes through the body
Up and over
The soggy cliff
An unwelcoming vibe
Overwhelming all emotions

Flashing bumpy line appears
Clearer as he gets closer
Anger fills over again
As he drops down into the heart of danger
Shoot one
Shoot two
This line is clear
Shoot three
Strike one with metal
One more sound
It all goes black.

Travis Grant Carree (13)
The St Leonards Academy, St Leonards-On-Sea

My Pet Rock

M y pet rock
Y ou may ask why, he's just a block

P rettily it sits, snug in my sock
E yeing at the clock
T ormenting just like a hawk

R idiculous, I don't care if you mock
O lly is his name and he's my rock
C aring and cold, he's the key to my lock
K illing my mind.

Tyler Reader (14)
The St Leonards Academy, St Leonards-On-Sea

You!

You, you, you,
You make me laugh all day
Just like the Milky Way
I love that you snore in your sleep
It makes me think of sheep

Your laugh is so precious
Especially when I'm nauseous
I want to celebrate your birthday
Because you were born on earth day
Out of all the people in the world
I'd always pick *you*.

Danny Smith (13)
The St Leonards Academy, St Leonards-On-Sea

Untitled

Fear me! I'm the burning, soul-devouring
Dismantling, destroying this pile of rusty rubble until it decays
Your hostility towards me is a score I have to settle
My golden flames that reach to the air like skyscrapers
With my misty smoke invading the innocents' nostrils
Until death comes for them
I hunger for hatred with a burning desire for revenge
Those who weep for freedom and for the mayhem to stop
Those are the ones who will die first
And soon be part of my wildfire
Spreading through this miserable city
The minds with a strong will are brave enough to enter my deadly gates of Hell
I'm a force who's insane
Uncanny and odd
But they still enter
One of them who escaped was free
But covered in the torched scars of my flames
My anger is so hot it blisters
You try to turn me to ash but it will never happen
Look me in the eyes and say your last goodbyes.

Blaise Watson (13)
The St Leonards Academy, St Leonards-On-Sea

World Of Music

Music transports me to a different world.
I love all the artists, boy or girl
I adore the melodies and all the amazing harmonies
I enjoy the way they seem to calm me
What I receive from music is inspiration
And I give all of my dedication
To the people who helped me to face my shyness
Or I would never be able to write this
Music transports me into a different world
When I listen I want to twirl
Music transports me into a different world
I love all the artists, boy or girl
Music is a forever flowing beautiful river
It is a forever lasting crown brushed in silver
It can be like a roaring lion
Strong and bold
But the notes like snowflakes
Always delicate to hold
Music transports me to a wonderful world
I love all the artists, boy or girl.

Kelsey Hayward (12)
The St Leonards Academy, St Leonards-On-Sea

The One I Loved . . .

The one I loved
The one I loved the most
He left me for the war
He stood up big and tall
Fought for his country
In the biggest war of all

The one I loved
The one I loved the most
He got us where we are today
All because he's brave
We miss you, we thank you
For all you have done
With that great big gun

The one I loved
The one I loved the most
Left me, for his life
The one I loved
The one I loved
Got struck by a knife.

Jordan Johns
The St Leonards Academy, St Leonards-On-Sea

Lasagne

Oh lasagne
Shall you be my meal for every night?
You are as crunchy as an earthquake crumbling
You make me feel so good, I love it, oh I love it
Despite that you are sometimes overcooked
But overlook the other food
You are as yellow as the sun beaming down on me
I wish I get to see you on the dinner table
Every night with your yellow glimmering skin
Oh I wish, oh I wish.

Christopher Morris (12)
The St Leonards Academy, St Leonards-On-Sea

My One And Only

You make my heart beat for a thousand miles
Every time I look at you, you make me smile
You are a ray of sunlight
To my dark and gloomy night

I will love you forever
Until we die
I see us growing old together
When I look into your eyes

Words can't describe how much I love you
But I'm gonna try
You make my life seem better
And you make my smile seem bigger

I adore you
A million stars in the sky
You're the one that shines in my eyes
You are my one and only
My one true love.

Manisha Jaanvi Ponnamperumage (13)
The St Leonards Academy, St Leonards-On-Sea

Sadness

(For my kitten, Poppy.)

I wish you were here with me,
Sometimes I wonder what life would be like if you were here.
I remember the days when we would play.

I sometimes cry because I miss you,
I love you so much
When I was sad you made me happy.

You mean the world to me,
You are so cute
I miss you and wish you were here
I would do anything to bring you back
You mean the world to me.

Georgina-May Milton (12)
The St Leonards Academy, St Leonards-On-Sea

Just A Little Angry

I'm just a little angry is what I thought
I just said I'm fine, well, that's what I got taught
What you can't really see, my brain tells me these things
But I know in my head that's not how it should be
I should say how I feel to whoever will listen
But people will judge so I keep my thoughts in my prison
I bottle it up then I try to throw it away
But it always comes back, day by day
I've seen a lot of things in life that I don't like to say
But it's made me this person that I am today
I know things will get better
I just need to pray
I'm just a little angry
These are just my teenage days.

Tanisha Smith
The St Leonards Academy, St Leonards-On-Sea

Goodbye My Angel

I could say I love you
Or I could say you are my world
I might wish to see you
Or I might ask for one last kiss

You were my everything
My one and only
When you smiled it brightened up my day
It makes me feel happy that you're watching over all of my choices

I could ask for a hug but never get one
I could love you forever and I will
I'll see you again when my time is up
The angels will take care of you now

But I will always love you
But for now you're safe in Heaven
So take care my angel
Sleep tight
And I wish to see you again.

Megan Louise Warren (12)
The St Leonards Academy, St Leonards-On-Sea

11:56, The 60 Seconds Of Death

The nation cries and wails
The world reacts with grief and pain
In a land so far away
I see people crying and
Some people do pray
The ground is erupting all around
People running – panic bound

Buildings are collapsing
People are buried
Hell on Earth – it really is horrid
How they died, how they survived
Only pain can tell, only eyes can dispel
Yes, it will never vanish, that sordid event
O world, they would have seen better days
Better times, better yesterdays
Before they fell into the arms of the debris and death.

Pranab Khadka (14)
The St Leonards Academy, St Leonards-On-Sea

Mine

A candle's departure obliterates every devoted love story
Whilst your deathly disquietude pains every bone in my love-aching body
I dread a loss
I gain a loss
As I cry in agony you slowly sacrilege my soul
Then you lacerate my irreparable heart
Before finally
My cry is no more
I hear your sorrowing cry of lament oscillate my mind
But your belated endearment
Will never be mine.

Emily Astell (13)
The St Leonards Academy, St Leonards-On-Sea

Joy For Football

You never know where to go
But when you are on the field
You suddenly know where to go
I feel like telling the world about a sport called football.
I must go on
If you don't care, go grab a scone
You run, walk but it's still fun.
Sit and watch or stand and say,
This is the way, so go and play
Don't forget, wear your boots
Or you'll get the boot!

Kelsey Boseley (12)
The St Leonards Academy, St Leonards-On-Sea

My Love

I love you so
That I can't let you go
You're the love of my life
The life is lost.

I never got to tell you how I felt
My feelings for you are unreal
And I would die for you
Because I love you.

You're the thing that's worth getting up for
When you smile you glow even more
And this is why I so dearly adore you.

Holly-Marie Gates (12)
The St Leonards Academy, St Leonards-On-Sea

Untitled

Silence!
I sit there alone
My eyes closed
My mind spinning around

Light closing in
My fears overcoming me
Empty!

The walls moving towards me
Will it stop?
Blankness
Searching for myself.

Jaya-Louise Griggs (13)
The St Leonards Academy, St Leonards-On-Sea

Waves Of Feelings

Feelings, you love 'em, you hate 'em
They are oceans of unpredictable emotion
They are invisible to the naked eye
They make you despise a spy's disguise
They make you adore the skies or love that one guy
That you'll be with for the rest of your life
Feelings they aren't all great
They can make you hate your mate
Even for one day, you lay on your bed
With these feelings in your head
Thinking *what have I just said?*
They're indecisive, do I like this guy?
Do I despise this guy?
Do I need this guy?
Feelings, you don't know what to do with them
Because they're not in your control
Do I let everybody know?
No, let them figure it out themselves!

Jamie David Bowyer (13)
The St Leonards Academy, St Leonards-On-Sea

The No-Faced Demons

One day in a magical castle
There lived a wizard called Professor Partel
He was bold and brave with lots of power
until late at night on this deathly hour
The weather was warm with a soft subtle breeze
Then a powerful wind brought shivering to his knees
The sky blackened with dark grey clouds
As the demons emerged and silenced all sound
The plants had frozen and turned as strong as steel
As the no-faced creatures swooped by like eels
The witches and wizards were forced to fight
Clutching their wands and begging to see daylight
'Wands at the ready!' the headmaster yelled
Hoping that they could defeat the demons with their magic spells
Now no one knew what happened to the castle
Or the powerful wizard, Professor Partel
But legend has it that once every year
In the Scottish mountains, his ghost will appear.

Leon Steven Robert Knowles (11)
The St Leonards Academy, St Leonards-On-Sea

School

Oh the school dinners are disgusting
They taste quiet revolting
The pizza tastes like cardboard
Why are people eating this?

Lessons are too short
Hope you don't get caught
Also breaks are short
As short as a glue stick

C3s are useless
Don't teach those bullies, it's pointless
They still carry on relentless
The victims, powerless
Work is hard
In fact, too hard
As hard as climbing a tower
Just let it go and work it out
Don't worry, don't pout.

Chris Chapman (14)
The St Leonards Academy, St Leonards-On-Sea

Frozen Desserts

Oh Maggie, your just deserts!
Are you still laughin' darlin'?
Pink strawberry stains of frozen desserts,
That greyhound growlin' and snarlin'.

So foolish, so mulish! Your skin still fair,
But dull with no sign of a blister,
Does ochre sun still run through your hair?
Still jealous of your sister?

Maggie, Maggie sipping red Bordeaux,
Eyes bruise-blue with damp frames of charcoal!
And her leather shoes, sashay to and fro
Red heels clacking to rock 'n' roll.

Maggie, Maggie time has healed your scar -
Though plenty more to discover!
Now take your bags and bid au revoir,
Goodbye bitter star-crossed lover.

Lana Griggs (13)
The St Leonards Academy, St Leonards-On-Sea

Delightful Strawberry

You are as delightful as the blue sky
With your cherry-red skin glimmering into the light
Sweet as sugar, your taste brings joy
Your smallness brings greatness
Which can't be penetrated by sadness
Strawberry, delightful, tasty strawberry
My lunches wouldn't be the same without you
Of you weren't in my life I'd die
Delightful strawberry, nothing comes close to your power
Nothing in the world
You are the food of the Lord's
Thankfully you are mine.

Chris Topliss (13)
The St Leonards Academy, St Leonards-On-Sea

The Bullied

Aimlessly I ran not using my mind
Not even checking if they were behind
I still could feel their harsh words raw
And the punch that had left me sore
The cause of me bolting out the door
And the tears as I fell to the dirty floor
I told my most supportive mum at home
Informed her how I felt alone
The school did nothing, I mean why should they care?
Kids will be kids, even when girls pull my long blonde hair
Here I was barely older than five
Wishing that I was no longer alive.

Kaia Andy Lonergan (14)
The St Leonards Academy, St Leonards-On-Sea

Government

The prime minister put Britain swimming in debt
But he's driving a Jaguar I bet
He wants to make a massive increase in tax
Poor people are angry but the 'suits' seem lax

They want to cut benefits by £8 billion
After reducing the NHS by £21 million
Lies and deceit to cover an agenda
Racism from UKIP will drive you round the bend
Conservatives winning the election is an issue
With Miliband's resignation, Labour needs a tissue
Last days before we lose more money
In cuts to the Conservative party.

Jordan Beeney (13)
The St Leonards Academy, St Leonards-On-Sea

Life In The Trenches

Life in the trenches was depressing and hard,
There were rats everywhere,
They were swimming through the thick mud,
Drowning in the flea-covered infectious vermin,
I saw shooting from a distance.

Life in the trenches was very bad,
I could hear the guns being fired,
Shooting from the trenches,
Approximately ten miles away,
All I could see, was smoke everywhere,
It filled the air,
It's like the war never ended.

Finlae Rose Sayle (11)
The St Leonards Academy, St Leonards-On-Sea

One More Lesson

She wanted to know
How to fly
To know why birds soar through the sky
She wanted to see what birds see
Learn how to be happy and free
He wanted to give up on life
To give up on the pain and the strife
He wanted to forget what he knew
For his good memories were few

She lent him her wings
So he could realise his blindness
Listen to the wonder which she sings
But he abused her kindness
He kept the feathers for himself
'You should have thought of yourself'
But it didn't matter, she said
And offered him one more lesson instead.

Ophelia Dickison (13)
The St Leonards Academy, St Leonards-On-Sea

Untitled

From the first moment I saw your face
My heart immediately skipped a beat
As my cheeks began to turn a deep shade of red
I realised that I was in love

I put on my make-up
And brushed my hair
And took one last look in the mirror
For a boy who would never care . . .

I see you at school
But I just hide behind my hair
Too scared to tell you
What I really feel

I've told my friends all about you
And they told me I should talk to you
So here I am walking up to you
I take a very weak breath . . .

Cordelia Jolley (14)
The St Leonards Academy, St Leonards-On-Sea

Let Me Be Free

I let them see smiles
Yet deep down inside
My heart is breaking
And I'm full of lies

No one knows the truth
Or the way I truly feel
I hold it all in
Like it's no big deal

There's one thing I want
And that's to be free
To spread my wings
And leap to safety

To let the truth come alive
And at last be free
Because that's who I want to be
I want to be me.

Mia Perigo Shoesmith (14)
The St Leonards Academy, St Leonards-On-Sea

This Is Alexandra Park

It's silent but loud
Wind is rushing through the air
Howling as it just skips me
It's warm, boiling
I'm sweating like mad
But I still have a smile on my face
It makes me happy to see all of the children playing
It's getting darker and darker
I go inside the cafe
All I see outside is a blanket of daisies growing over the grass
The trees are so big they leave massive shadows behind every step
Under it you get cooler and cooler
The fountain is beautiful
It's surrounded by fresh growing roses
They stand like bodyguards
Birds just relax in the cool blue water
This is Alexandra Park . . .

Beth Anne Percy (12)
The St Leonards Academy, St Leonards-On-Sea

Nepal's Earthquake

Crash! Bang! Smash!
The buildings are turning rusty
Nepal has began to get dusty
The people feel despair
Nepal needs a repair

Most of the bodies have started to rot
Where it all happened
Beneath the bottom
The floors have started to rise
When all the undead are filling with flies
There's nothing left to be built
Because of the earthquake, everything's started to tilt.

Charles William Russell (13)
The St Leonards Academy, St Leonards-On-Sea

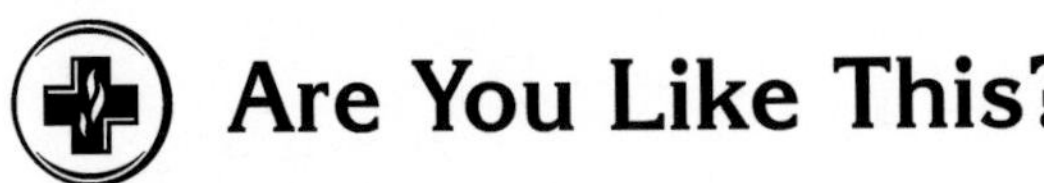

Are You Like This?

You are sweet and kind
You're generous to people!
You smell like cookies
You look like a green summer's day!
You're like butterflies
As beautiful as flowers!

As gentle as love
As perfect as perfection!
As cute as puppies
Delicious chocolate cake
As special as friends
We are the best forever.

Carrie Benge (11)
The St Leonards Academy, St Leonards-On-Sea

My Feeling

A tree reaching for the clouds
Or the blooming of flowers
Screaming your secrets out loud
Or the sense of magical powers
That's my feeling
That's my feeling

Hearing the sounds of singing birds
Or being with you holding hands
Listening to soft sweet words
Or making ridiculous plans
That's my feeling
That's my feeling.

Jade Ye (13)
The St Leonards Academy, St Leonards-On-Sea

Red Rose

I held this fragile rose
Close with greatest embrace
Often looking and staring at it
Forgetting my current displace

The soft texture of the petal
As my fingers graze
Upon its delicate surface
I glare, amazed

As time passed by
They began to fade
Silence poured out
And all types of coloured shades.

Chloe Bolingbroke (14)
The St Leonards Academy, St Leonards-On-Sea

The Room That Was Not!

The room was full of silence
The room was full of noise
The room could not be explained
As the room wasn't there

The room with walls that poured with blood
The room with black darkening windows
The room with no soil or life
The room that silenced the air

The room that could make your eyeballs pop
The room that would crush your soul and mind
The room that made horrible noises
That would spread devastation

The room was never really a room
The room was unexplainable
The room could tear you apart but
There was never a room just nothing.

Joshua Guest (14)
The St Leonards Academy, St Leonards-On-Sea

KFC

KFC, oh KFC
I might get fat
But you're so tasty
So I don't care about that

I love your ten piece bucket
Or the £1.99 snack box
It's so delicious
I think it rocks

Getting my face dirty
In all that grease
It's the best feeling ever
It feels like a feast

Take KFC to Christmas
It's gonna be loved
If someone really hates it
Then smack them with a glove.

John Soltana (14)
The St Leonards Academy, St Leonards-On-Sea

Best Friends

Jade, she is my best friend
We have our ups and downs
She is always there for me
We are good friends
We love the same food
We both have pets
No one can take us apart
No matter what happened
We disagree on a lot of things
We sometimes annoy each other
That's why we are friends
She will always be beside me
And I will always be beside her
I will never hurt her
And she will never hurt me
We will always be friends
For the rest of our lives.

Amy Langley (14)
The St Leonards Academy, St Leonards-On-Sea

I Walked Through The Park

I walked through the huge park
Where ducks quack and dogs bark
Kids play throughout the day
And parents say, 'What a beautiful day'
The sun is out, standing tall
And leaves fall barely at all
People shout, without no doubt
But me, I walk having fun
Feeding ducks and filling their tum
Giving them yummy bread
Keeping them full until they go to bed
The seagulls scream at the top of their voice
While people make the right choice
Going outside and enjoying the sun
Playing games and having fun
But me, I walk through the park
Remembering this day until it gets dark.

Harry Hammond (12)
The St Leonards Academy, St Leonards-On-Sea

Oh Gem!

I love that you shine in the light
You are pretty and smooth like silk
When you shine you make me smile
You make me smile when I'm sad
Your beautiful shape is my gem

I want to celebrate the way you shine
I want to rejoice about your shape
I want to tell the world how amazing you are

I love your shape
I love your colour
And most of all I love you
I will never change you.

Chloe Wright (13)
The St Leonards Academy, St Leonards-On-Sea

Anger

Anger runs through my blood each day
It makes me angry when people barge past me
I lose my temper too much for me to calm
Fighting for destiny is hard in life for someone like me

I want to change but I can't
I want to change my temper but I can't
I want to change my life but I can't
Would you change your temper if you were like me?

When I am angry I feel like an erupting volcano
Are you like that?
Do you lose your temper
Do you hate the way you live your life?

Celia Potter (14)
The St Leonards Academy, St Leonards-On-Sea

Favourite Place

Oh!
I love that delightful place where I often go
And the delightful privacy that follows
Where I am, there I peacefully drift off into my thoughts
To the sky, to the clouds, to Heaven's gates
Before the hands of reality guide me home

I want the world to know how fabulously
Ferociously, fantastic my favourite place is
I want to celebrate the peaceful secrecy of my place
I want to stay there for all eternity

I love the smells of my favourite place
I love the sights of my favourite place.

April Clemett (14)
The St Leonards Academy, St Leonards-On-Sea

The Flaming Arrow

The fear is red like a flaming arrow
Flying through the sky
It tastes like I was reborn
It smells like dead zombies
Trying to attack the town
It looks like the walking dead is coming to life
It feels like something bad
Like madness and it sounds like destruction.

Have you been so angry?
I know bad
I know sad
I know harsh
But I'll survive.

Albert Mazurek (12)
The St Leonards Academy, St Leonards-On-Sea

Save Nepal

Just the typical daybreak, yet
Soon their town would shake
Soon their houses would fall apart
And leave them all with a broken heart
Save Nepal,
Normal day, normal people
Expecting nothing awful
Come on let's be smart
Nepal is being pulled apart
Save Nepal
The tremors beginning,
Began to spread fear
The earth was crying and shedding tears.
The earthquake had finished its start
Nepal was starting to fall apart
Save Nepal,
Save Nepal!

Charlie Kent (13)
The St Leonards Academy, St Leonards-On-Sea

Riding Through Nature

Galloping through the woods
Trees as green as gems
Jumping over the logs
Ouch, the floor is hard!

Galloping through the fields
Jumping over rivers
Rivers as blue as the sky

Walking along the sand
The sand pulling us closer to the sea
Walking in the water
Very refreshing, not getting too hot

Time to go home
A slow walk back
The sun starting to go down
Trying to remember the way home.

Liam Aird (14)
The St Leonards Academy, St Leonards-On-Sea

World Of Racism

Racism must stop!
Fighting for human rights
Filled with rage as this carries on
Why do we ignore racism?

Racism should stop
Fury, rage and horror as I see this carry on
It makes me angry when I see racism
Why do we ignore racism?

How can we allow this to carry on?
Disgraceful as we are all creatures of society
What has anyone done about racism?
Nothing, because no one cares about it
I want to change how people feel about racism.

Frankie Sollo (13)
The St Leonards Academy, St Leonards-On-Sea

DJ Mixing

Turn tables, keyboards, CDJs and computers
All inside one booth
Stick a USB port in the tooth of a CDJ
Feel the vibe of the crowd
Mix from a USB port

Vinyl records don't have cue buttons
All they have are cueing stickers
Cue finds part of a song
Soon of which that part of the song is gone

Frankie Knuckles, Todd Edwards, MK and Patrick Topping's sounds
Are at the popping of good sounds
Ten Walls and Max Cooper's sounds can be a little quiet
With the voice of electronic and ambient music.

Fergus Strickland
The St Leonards Academy, St Leonards-On-Sea

Show Them

Fury, rage, horror
My body steamed with anger
I can't bear it anymore
How can I allow this?
Let's show our fists
Let's show our skill
Let's show them how we fight
I want change
I want change
Why do we ignore?
We aren't this poor
I want change
I want change
I want change.

Tommy Lyons (13)
The St Leonards Academy, St Leonards-On-Sea

Hopefully I Can Satisfy You!

I'm not rich this is true
But maybe I can satisfy you
I once loved in Lanzarote
To come back, where the weather's grotty
At the age of seven I wanted a snake
Which my mum did not appreciate
As for school I did not rule
I sat in the corner and looked like a fool
Hush, hush now, this ain't quite over
Who am I, Casanova?
I recently just turned twelve today
And got a tarantula, hip hip hooray
Bye, everybody, toodledoo
Hopefully I have satisfied you.

Chloe Macnicol (12)
The St Leonards Academy, St Leonards-On-Sea

Hell Riots

Crash
Fire and flames roar up to the sky
Thunder and lightning roar into the city
Hell returns to the heavens
Police stand
One by one, stamping feet
Stamp, stamp, stamp
Police stand up straight with arms at point
Clouds of black dust rise, to the hell of people's anger
Rumbling, the ground shakes with might
Enemy falls to the cold hard ground
People thrown around
Slam, slam, slam
The fleet of vans rumble out of the city
Blearing down the street
With the hell of anger within them.

Philip Young (13)
The St Leonards Academy, St Leonards-On-Sea

Yet It's Always Dominic's Side

O the annoyance of my brother
Always getting me grounded.
The howl of his voice
'Mum, Mum, Mum, *Mummm!*
Erika punched me!'
And she always believed him.
The thoughts I have are horrendous
How I wish he wasn't here
Occasionally I'll call him 'Dustbin Boy'
But he always tells on me.

She'll always ground me
And say I can't go anywhere
I tell her why I do it
But yet it's always Dominic's side

Yet it's always Dominic's side!

Erika Williams (13)
The St Leonards Academy, St Leonards-On-Sea

Hospital Antics

C urse, slaughter and pain
R unning, trying to get away
O nly they can help
H appiness is sometimes a distant memory
N o one can help but them
S adness, sadness, sadness

D anger can be as delicate as glass
I gnorance is present
S ometimes I feel the churning of death
E ating may be forbidden
A t times it gets better
S ometimes I feel like it's over
E ndless days of being a teenager.

Adam Double (13)
The St Leonards Academy, St Leonards-On-Sea

The Kid In The Mirror

The humility and shame in my eyes
I deserve the lowest amount of appreciation
My soul is a mistake
Why always me?

Not even good enough for the term 'four eyes'
Pity to others around
Unwanted, unnecessary, unselected
To never be wanted
Brushes, brushes, brushes
Sitting alone in the corner
To never be wanted

Lowest of the low
Bullied by the bullies
Respect gone through the roof
Parents showing disregard.

Billy Kennedy-Carr (13)
The St Leonards Academy, St Leonards-On-Sea

Cars

Oh cars,
I love that you are something to me
You are magnificent and gifted to me
When you drive past me, I smile my face off
You make me thrilled and I can't complain
You're seriously something, I can't change you
Oh cars
When you come past me your engines are like tigers' roars!
And I want to tell the world how amazing you are to me
You make me fly high into the sky
Oh cars
I love the way you are
I love the sound you make
And most of all I love the way you look.

Ryan Oak (14)
The St Leonards Academy, St Leonards-On-Sea

I Feel A Spirit

God is in Heaven
He has created the world
Let us worship Him
My favourite place
Is Heaven
Most of all I love God
And the angels above
Jesus died on the Cross
We are all His children
We should read the Bible
Go to church every Sunday
Eat bread and drink wine
Blood was spilt
Baptism happens only once
Praise God!

Tyler Bazeley (13)
The St Leonards Academy, St Leonards-On-Sea

Untitled

I could say friendship's weird
But it can be good
The laughs people have
The upsets people have
But that's why you should have friends.

When you feel happy or sad
Your friends will be there
You will bond and fight
And have emotional times

I could say friendship's weird
But it can be a close friendship
Losing friendships
Making new friendships
But that is why we all have friends.

Abbie Turner (13)
The St Leonards Academy, St Leonards-On-Sea

Happy Place

The sky was clear and scorching hot
A place that horses like to trot
Golden sand as soft as akin
And water that emotionally runs away
Children jumping over the waves
With mums telling them to behave
The reflective light shines in my eyes
On the perfect beach
People walking in their socks
As they cross the terrible rocks
Happy laughs across the path
Kids with ice creams
As they play in little streams
The one place everyone will smile
On the cheerful beach.

Chloe Wilson
The St Leonards Academy, St Leonards-On-Sea

Fear

My parents argue and raise their voices
I ask so much for them to stop
I try so hard not to listen
But it's too loud to block
Don't bring me up like this
Mum, Dad just watch me grow up
Before it's too late
They ensure it's OK by a kiss
I go upstairs and shut the door
They find me asleep on the floor
My hands tightly forced to my ears
They realise this is one of my biggest fears
Family is all that I need
Why put me in this position?

Liberty Begbie (14)
The St Leonards Academy, St Leonards-On-Sea

The Other Side

No one knows how hard it is
How stressful, how sad
I'm from somewhere far away
I used to live in New Zealand, the other side
A land made from smiles and dreams
Where I had happy, long, sunny days
And countless friends by my side
But that's all gone now
I'm alone here in England
No one really likes me
Mum says she knows,
Dad says he knows
How hard it is
They don't, I do.

Daisy Leitch (12)
The St Leonards Academy, St Leonards-On-Sea

If It's Angels You Want

If it's angels you want
You can have as many as you like
But, do not take mine
My dear, my precious
Wrath can't explain
Rage can't explain
Nothing can explain the spear piercing through
You took him from my grasp
He was mine, my own
The flames engulfed, as you reached
The smoke choked, as you took
If it's angels you want
You can have as many as you like
But do not take mine.

Rebecca Stevens (14)
The St Leonards Academy, St Leonards-On-Sea

My Console Friend

Oh!
I love that game
And the PSP
Oh I wonder his name
Who could it be?
You keep me up a while
When will it end?
Who could leave you
Alone for a while?
You are a king
You help me when I'm down
When it's shutting down
I always say goodbye.

Yves Thursfield (11)
The St Leonards Academy, St Leonards-On-Sea

Dark Lies

My mind is filled with darkness, terror fills my body
The more lies, the less marks, the graves shiver
How can the darkness get so realistic?
So many times I've tried to be happy and smile
My real smile is trapped inside me
The only way you will make smiles
Is hold me down or tell me sad, little lies
When rain pours down my face in the blackness
The tears of my horror scream in fear
But no one can hear the loud cries
When the time is right shadows will turn light
Cries will turn into laughs, my memories will be free
Don't worry Mummy, I will be free, my spirit will live on.

Rebekka Ashcroft (14)
The St Leonards Academy, St Leonards-On-Sea

The Amazing Memory

The memory of this place was amazing
Wonderful and uplifting
Staring out at the sparkling diamond sea
The sunset brings us night
The memory of this place was amazing
Looking forward at loving people, they cherish and love one another
I stand tall, I stand firm, I stand frozen here
The memory of this place is amazing
I still stand here unable to move
Watching the stars glitter and glow
While everyone sleeps
I may not move, but I see all, remember all
This place is, and will always be, amazing.

Pip Stevens (14)
The St Leonards Academy, St Leonards-On-Sea

Chocolate

I love that smell
That invades my nostrils of delight,
Delight that can be heard as loud as a bell,
You taste so nice that you're gone in a click of a light,
The milky taste of your sensation
Fills the nation
With joy.
Oh chocolate,
You are as good tasting and good looking,
However, you are as precious as a diamond,
And better tasting than an almond.
Oh chocolate,
We love your taste that could fill the nation.

Cameron Jenkins (11)
The St Leonards Academy, St Leonards-On-Sea

The Black Beauty

The hooves pounding on the ground
As the rider came back around to jump the fence
The beautiful black stallion is snorting onto the hard concrete
After a good hack and jump
He eats a huge lump of molly chaff and pony nuts
His smooth fur that runs through your hand
This animal has no fear, like a lion
The hooves beat into the ground
That night wasn't the best of nights
The rain crashed on the metal
It rusted away leaving holes which made the stallion depressed
His soaking wet fur sticks to your hand
You'll never meet a stallion like this.

Kimberley Hills
The St Leonards Academy, St Leonards-On-Sea

Lost Little Boy

One winter evening me and my dad
Went to find some food
It was a horrible, windy and rainy day
I met with a young little boy
But my dad did not realise
I went after him
It was beginning to be morning
I started to be worried
My tears slowly dripped and dripped down my face
I could hear his voice whisper in my ear
He sounded like a ghost
I was cold, I was tired
I just wanted to be at home.

Patrik Pergel
The St Leonards Academy, St Leonards-On-Sea

Oh! Sweet Cake

Oh! My dearest cake
Your succulent strawberries are embedded into your icing
A beautiful and sugary sticky pale brown
Your sponge is light, luscious and lifting
While the smell of your deliciousness is chocolaty
Along with the most divine taste
Cake, oh cake, how I love thee
You make my desserts complete
Your chocolate toppings drizzled, draped and dropped
Oh cake
You simply are the best
You're like heaven but better
Oh cake, let me eat you!

Jess Harrison
The St Leonards Academy, St Leonards-On-Sea

Ode To United

O United
I love that you are such an awesome team
You are brave and strong,
Your skills ignited
When you hit the net we scream
You make the crowd excited
Your players are supreme
I want to celebrate the way Reds pass
I want to rejoice about your dream
I want to tell the world of your class
I love the crowd
We shout out loud
And most of all you make me proud.

Evan Crang (13)
The St Leonards Academy, St Leonards-On-Sea

The Strongest Love

The water rippled blue
And the grass is crystal green
I stare through the hazy hue
And search for the unseen
The delicate drops of rain
That cling to every leaf
The powerful lion that shakes its mane
A cunning thief
The moon twinkles in the night
And the sun dazzles us in the day
A fading light that shows me the way
The solitary shaft of light that shines through
These are the things that remind me of you . . .

Amouna Soltana (13)
The St Leonards Academy, St Leonards-On-Sea

The Nepal Earthquake

Did you hear
The shocking news about the Nepal earthquake?
It's faced with horror and destruction
This concerns me about the lives that have been lost
I wonder how they could have survived?
As they must have tried
Especially the climbers on Mount Everest
Must have been serious
As I think it must have been hideous
This is serious and I'm curious
Of how big the monstrous avalanche was
Now people will starve and have nowhere to bath
So donate a pound and help them be saved.

Harrison Crocker (12)
The St Leonards Academy, St Leonards-On-Sea

Strong

Look into my eyes
What do you see?
I'm not that happy, cheerful girl you think you see
Instead I'm that girl who lives with self-hatred
I'm drowning in my own tears
But you never realised . . .
The feeling of betrayal
Why do you make me hide
My fear deep inside
I've learned not to trust
I could never forgive you
I want to thank you though
Because in reality you made me stronger.

Millie Barnes (14)
The St Leonards Academy, St Leonards-On-Sea

Angel Of Light

Sweet serenity
Peace and blessing
Poise with equanimity
Wholehearted and devoted
Assertive and joyful
Angel of God, a custodian with a watchful eye,
She had an angular posture and was draped in
White garments embellished with a shimmering gold,
As a trusted protector,
Defender against sins.
Carrying a bouquet of garnet-red flowers flecked with white,
Wings flapping and golden hair whipping the wind
She tends them and cares for them under the holy golden light.

Felicity Stewart (12)
The St Leonards Academy, St Leonards-On-Sea

Stop, Think

Save Nepal, don't give up
Your money will go to a good cause
When people come to your house
For money don't just slam your doors

Stop, think, look at what we have here
Spend for poor Nepal not for an ice-cold beer

Stop, think, think about the child,
They deserve a house that's nice and neat
Not one that looks all wild.

Stop, think!

Daunté Moses Dominique Cherubin (12)
The St Leonards Academy, St Leonards-On-Sea

Untitled

Shaking, drifting
Devastation, shifting
Awful power, destroying, forthwith
Disaster, disaster, April 25th

Centuries of history, gone overnight
Swallowing lives, they can't win this fight
Nothing left, nothing to say, it isn't a myth
Disaster, disaster, April 25th

The East has been ravaged by the power of a tempest
Forever remember the quake that shook Everest
Pray for Nepal, pay your tithe
Disaster, disaster, April 25th.

David Nyss (14)
The St Leonards Academy, St Leonards-On-Sea

Football

The thing I love is football,
Many people enjoy it
But many people don't!
Football is not just about winning and scoring goals.

I think it should be celebrated, not hated.
The atmosphere is amazing inside a stadium,
The roar of the crowd is like a lawn mower being started
So it can rip the grass to shreds.

Outside of a stadium is just as good
The smell of the greasy chips and burgers or hot dogs
Makes a wonderful feeling in your nose
It almost makes you crave that type of food!

Reece Lincoln (12)
The St Leonards Academy, St Leonards-On-Sea

Self-Harm

She paints her pretty picture
But her canvas is her wrist
While her paintbrush has a twist

She paints her pretty picture
As she tells her story
And the emotions crawl out

She paints her pretty picture
While the pain like tears thunder out
And her canvas gets deeper

And deeper and deeper
Until her knife just drops.

Hollie Lil Fitzgerald (14)
The St Leonards Academy, St Leonards-On-Sea

Day Down The Beach

As I run on the sand
The warmth between my toes
My crispy wet hair, that's how it goes

I hear the seagulls squawk
Whilst all the children talk
And the warmth hits my cheeks

People skimming stones
And others going home
And ice cream being sold on the beach

It then feels like home
And I never want to go back to the old street.

Molly Swaine (13)
The St Leonards Academy, St Leonards-On-Sea

Rioting

Poor people not having homes
Should stop!
Racism
Must stop!
Filled with rage
I need to demonstrate
Fury
Rage
Horror
Fills my body
I want change
In my life.

Samuel Stimson (12)
The St Leonards Academy, St Leonards-On-Sea

Old Hill Of Hastings

The old little train keeps going up the hill
Still with the memories of when we went up when I was a little kid
But now everything has changed as the town gets busier
More people use the train and the hill is busier
But there is something which is the same, the red ice cream van
Lots of children smile when they have the ice cream in their hands
But when the birds get their ice cream they start to get upset and some start to cry
There are lots of birds up there in the hill, most of them sit on the ice cream van
And just wait to get the ice cream for children
But what could happen next?

Finley Clark
The St Leonards Academy, St Leonards-On-Sea

Why Did You Wait?

Frozen in mind
Repeated in seconds
Green eyes, olive skin, you praise the reflection
The words held qualities laced with perfection
Disguise is your masterpiece, filled with misconception
Homebound to hell before she knew . . .
What it was she battled through
Ten years you had to change but your honour was placed high in your name
Cut her nose off to spite face
The window to her trust left behind an empty space
She waits for that is all she has known
And she waits.

Alexandria Stringfellow (13)
The St Leonards Academy, St Leonards-On-Sea

I Could

I could say the sun is out
Or I could say the sun is like a moon
I might tell you the sun is bright
Or I might say it's beautiful
You are a shadow
You are beautiful
When you're with me
It makes me feel happy
I could look at the sky
I could see the stars
I might think of you
Or I might just dream.

Charlotte Gibb (14)
The St Leonards Academy, St Leonards-On-Sea

Me

Me
My life
It's a mess
They don't know how to care for me
They don't know how to talk to me
Why do they do this?
Why don't people listen?
I ask a question . . . no answer
What is so good about that monster?
That evil, no good monster
It doesn't care about anything but you
How would you feel if you were me?

Rachel Old (14)
The St Leonards Academy, St Leonards-On-Sea

The Worries Of War . . .

Bang, as the bullet hits the floor
Bang, as the bomb explodes the door
Young girls and young boys
Have to be evacuated and leave their toys
Crying and wondering why things are so mad
Wondering if they will ever see their mum and their dad
Families receiving the worst news of their life
Their son, dad or husband has been attacked with a knife
They put down the phone and the clouds are now grey
All they can do now is hope and pray
The children are crying, flooding with tears
When will this stop? It's been going on for years.

Lily Georgia Rose Bloomfield (13)
The St Leonards Academy, St Leonards-On-Sea

He Follows

I awoke from the soaking mud
Place unknown
Attempting to lift my numb legs, where am I?
I look around, trees and darkness
These voices, who are they?
I see a page attached to a tree
'Always watches'
I grab the note, holding it close
Something lurks behind me, I turn in fear
The voices, become vivid
'He's coming, don't look'
I can see him now. Slender.

Harley Mason Roberts (14)
The St Leonards Academy, St Leonards-On-Sea

Loneliness

I am the blue overcoming your body
The wave of salty tears rolling down your face
I am the break in your heart, shatter, crack
The break which can't be fixed
I am the smell of sorrow,
Like the sea on a dark and cold night
I am the quiet girl in the corner of the room
The girl drowning in her own tears, *drip, drip, drip . . .*
The girl who sees children, families in happiness
I am the feeling, the shiver of the loneliness
I am the sound of laughter and
You know you may never laugh again.

Jessica Ellen Avery (12)
The St Leonards Academy, St Leonards-On-Sea

Seafront

Walking along the salty seafront
Wild wind hits you in the fragile face
People fishing and having a great time

Suddenly you smell the amazing fish and chips
Walking along the beach trying to find
The delightful shop
You walk into the shop
You see the outstanding ice cream Mr Whippy

As you sit watching the waves touching the stones
And they gently get pulled in
Then you think for a bit and then you say, 'I'm complete.'

Daisy Churchyard (12)
The St Leonards Academy, St Leonards-On-Sea

Oh! Summer

You are as magical as Narnia in the beautiful snow,
How I love the summer rain, the lemonade stands
The long, lingering daylight hours that go by so slowly.

You are as precious to me as a squirrel with its acorns
With your amazing sunsets and summertime songs
I love the braided hair, I love the colourful flavoured slushes
From the smell of freshly cut grass
To the feeling of warm sea breeze on my cheek

You come and go so quickly
When you are not here I long for your return
Oh how I love summer!

Megan Green
The St Leonards Academy, St Leonards-On-Sea

Too Many Days I Have Waited For You

Too many days I have waited for you
Reminiscing your rich, silky, hazel eyes
And how tranquil we lay beneath the cloudless skies
This emptiness and chill I feel inside
Not a pearl
Nor a diamond
Can seal my affection
I pray for the day when we can meet again
When I can feel the presence of your perfection
To be yours and never feel the pain.

Sadie Bond (13)
The St Leonards Academy, St Leonards-On-Sea

Is It A Nightmare Or Is It A Dream?

I've been thinking about my life and why it's so horrible
Sometimes I feel life is miserable
I've always wondered why I was born?
Trying to make my feelings heard is like a duck mowing a lawn
No one knows what it's like to be me
Reflecting on every possibility
Have you ever felt like the world is closing in?
Becoming a teenager is the worst ever thing
Will my nightmare ever become a dream?
And by the way, I'm twelve not thirteen!

Tyra Hoad (12)
The St Leonards Academy, St Leonards-On-Sea

Pizza

Pizza, oh pizza
I love you so
You're my favourite Italian food
But I feel guilty eating you
Your crispy crust that flakes in my mouth
You're an oozing mountain of cheese
You're great with chips, the perfect pair
I love you with ketchup too!
Pizza, dear pizza
What would I do without you?
I don't know!

Amy Moule (14)
The St Leonards Academy, St Leonards-On-Sea

Terror Caused By Brother

I get annoyed, I have anger
And I get annoyed because of my brother
Living with him has been rough, even when he acts tough
It makes me angry when there is loads of shouting
But all I do is start ignoring
Fury, rage and horror in my room
When I get angry that will be doom
My father says, 'Control your temper'
And that's something I will always remember
I believe that I have lost my mind
And that is why I am not kind.

Thomas Wilson (11)
The St Leonards Academy, St Leonards-On-Sea

Excitement

Loud screams
I heard loud screams
I felt the excitement of other girls
When they hear your songs
Your music is incredible
I want to tell the world
How amazing your songs are
They love your music
They love your songs
And most of all they love your singing
Their excitement will never end.

Kelsie Glover (12)
The St Leonards Academy, St Leonards-On-Sea

Sadness

Sadness is a teardrop
When no one cares
You end up crying
It's like a footstep walking away
I'm on my own
Always let down
I am a river flowing
I look like a dark cloud
No one here to make you happy
Anxiety, anxiety makes you sad
Sadness makes you feel bad.

Stephanie Warner (12)
The St Leonards Academy, St Leonards-On-Sea

Mountain Top

Halfway up a gigantic, snowy mountain
I try my best to reach the top
I gradually turn my head to the side
To see the trees covered in snow
I could not take my eyes off the glimmering snow
As it sparkles in my eyes
Not paying much attention
I slip down the mountain top
On the floor gazing into the white, fluffy clouds
I wonder what happened
Will I be OK?

Kieron Ward (14)
The St Leonards Academy, St Leonards-On-Sea

Fire Child

Fury, rage and horror
He was fighting for where he lived
Flames were up in the air and sure to scare
Orange and red surrounded the young boy
But wait, he remembered his sister
She was sitting on a fire
Her skin melted away into ashes
'Nooo,' the child was crying and crying
However he found something shiny
With a bullet or two
Then there was a loud *bang!*

Ryan Graham Lucas (12)
The St Leonards Academy, St Leonards-On-Sea

I Am The Bountiful Ballot Box

I am the decisive hand that descends
I am the ever-changing result
I am the aftermath
I am the problems
I am the victories
I am the factions ferociously at war
I am the aftermath
You are the people
You decide who seizes power
You decide who comes up short
I am the result!

Ben Jacobs (14)
The St Leonards Academy, St Leonards-On-Sea

See You Again

Across the Mississippi river
Past the almighty snake that slithers
Alongside the great oak tree
For that door you need a key
A little girl has cotton candy
A wallet for my money can be handy
This is all the things I remember from my dad
If he was here he would be glad
However, he isn't which makes me sad
I need to tell lots of good news
When I see you again.

Roy Hughes (14)
The St Leonards Academy, St Leonards-On-Sea

Being Something Else

I've been thinking about what it's like
To be someone else
What it's like being someone else
What it's like being different
I wonder what it would be like
If someone else could be me?
Have you felt like you want to be someone else?
Trying to make my feelings heard isn't easy
Imagine if you were me
How would you feel?
No one knows, no one knows.

Shakira Louise Helsdown (13)
The St Leonards Academy, St Leonards-On-Sea

Oh Darling!

Oh darling
You shine brighter than the sun
With your beautiful golden hair
Flowing through the air
I love your features and the sound of your laughter
Even all the mystical creatures
Cannot be as beautiful as the sound of your laughter
Oh darling, oh darling
Nothing can compare to you, nothing at all
You are the queen of queens
With more than magical beans.

Luana Maffei (14)
The St Leonards Academy, St Leonards-On-Sea

The Lonely Girl

She was a normal girl, she sat on her own
With no one to talk to
And no one to cry at.
But she had the same people every day.

The next day I looked around
But she was nowhere to be seen,
In no corner, in no place.

I went to her house,
No girl was there
But there were two devastated parents.

Paige-Marie Barnard
The St Leonards Academy, St Leonards-On-Sea

Beloved Cake

Creamy, bubbly, fluffy, light
This is the thing that brings such delight!
It makes me feel like I'm in Heaven
It's my beloved gorgeous possession

When you put it in the oven, it is really rather stubborn
It moves around and rises, bubbles, it does nothing but cause trouble
But in the end, nothing can beat
Its scrumptious layers, it's amazing to eat!
Nothing can ever be replaced, by its taste bud-tingling taste!
Oh mighty cake, will you be my date?

Libby Caitlyn Mitchell (12)
The St Leonards Academy, St Leonards-On-Sea

Emotions

Change
Needed
Raging roar
Fury, lies, tears
Arguing, bribery, frightening fears

Screaming, shouting, fed up of arguing
I'm leaving soon
Gone into
Explode
Mode.

Sarah Elizabeth Graham (14)
The St Leonards Academy, St Leonards-On-Sea

Thief Of Life

When I consider my life
For every day I wish for a knife
To cut the pain
I could be a pane of glass
I feel like I'm chagrin
As if I'm a sin
But I'm surrounded by bars
I only wish there were stars
Out of this hell
Into a white cell.

Joe Chapman (13)
The St Leonards Academy, St Leonards-On-Sea

Lies

I am trying to be defensive
While you're being aggressive
The feeling of denial
What have I done wrong?
You're making me want to be suicidal
Why do you make me hide
My feelings deep inside
You told me I was living a lie
You told me you no longer care
You told me not to cry.

Lewis Speer (14)
The St Leonards Academy, St Leonards-On-Sea

The Empty Hearse

It doesn't matter how you die
On the lifeline getting hit with bullets made of lead
Unless, unless you live a life of lie
Then no matter what you do, you're still dead
It's very easy and it's very quick
And trust me it's very peaceful up here
The only thing is you need to know how to do the trick
To watch the sad faces of the ones you hold dear
And soon they will die, stinky old you
They won't even get to know the sad, sad truth.

Jessica Clemett (12)
The St Leonards Academy, St Leonards-On-Sea

Terrible Teenager Times

I've been thinking about society and how much they judge me
When I consider committing suicide
I stop and think then close my eyes . . .
Reflecting on who I will hurt inside
Sometimes I feel confused and hurt
But then I remember how hard I've worked.
Have you ever felt like a fish out of water?
When the waves start crashing and your life gets harder?
Being a teenager is sometimes confusing
But with the right attitude it could be amusing.

Katy Smith (13)
The St Leonards Academy, St Leonards-On-Sea

Untitled

Bang!
Bullets whistle through the angry sky
Injecting fear to all the towns and cities
Lightning strikes as loud as a dinosaur roars
Chasing into bombs of hell on all the rooftops
Babies' tears flood for miles
Dismantled buildings sway into the distance
Blazing fire swans around decaying through flesh and bones
Hearts full of despair
Wishing it will end.

Natalie Goodrum (14)
The St Leonards Academy, St Leonards-On-Sea

The Day Of Friday

Fridays
Why do I love you so?
Why, because I do, because you're the last day
Because you're a day of easiness
Every day I count the days, every hour
Every minute and every second
You are like a quest, to find a volcano full of gold
Every day, when I wake up on Friday
I feel as happy as winning the lottery
Oh Friday, I love you so.

Rian Giles (14)
The St Leonards Academy, St Leonards-On-Sea

Run

Wind in my face
Heart racing, keep the pace
Finish line in sight
Trophy shining so bright
Everyone so far
I feel like the star
Tearing through the ribbon
I hope I am forgiven
For I have won
Like the burning sun.

Abbie May Barfield (12)
The St Leonards Academy, St Leonards-On-Sea

My Grandma

Every day has been a struggle
It's been a year and it's still hard to believe that you are gone
Sometimes I don't know what to do with myself
Days where I don't want to get out of bed
Days where I just want to sit and cry
I miss your smile
I miss your voice
And all your comforting ways
You will always belong in my heart
Forever . . .

Megan Hood (12)
The St Leonards Academy, St Leonards-On-Sea

Love Is Forever

Every time I think of you
I feel the intensity
Of loving you
Like you could never imagine
What I want more than anything
Is to hold you tight and never let go
And tell you just how much you mean to me
I want you in my life for infinity
Love lasts forever
Hopefully with you.

Daisy Earl (13)
The St Leonards Academy, St Leonards-On-Sea

Corruption

Our world is filled with corruption
You can chase after the light but soon you'll realise
It's non-existent
Our world is the definition of destruction
All the politicians
Say that they will make the world better
But they can't keep that promise
Our world is twisted
You could be the one to change it
If you're committed.

Sarthak Rai (12)
The St Leonards Academy, St Leonards-On-Sea

Untitled

I wipe a tear from my eye
I wish I had the love
The anger comes when I see you with her
Then I start to cry because of you
You were the sunshine to me
But now it's shattered away because of you
I want it to fade away but it won't go
I wanted to tell you but I couldn't
You were a lightning in my head
But now disappear into thin air.

Sacha Hughes White (13)
The St Leonards Academy, St Leonards-On-Sea

Earthquake Terror

Did you hear there was an earthquake in Nepal?
Their world has been turned upside down
People desperately need help
Our country urgently needs to help
What will happen if there is not enough help?
They sadly have no food, home or water
If we don't act quickly they will die.
They will die as quickly as I crunch leaves on the ground.
Poor parents have been sadly separated from loved ones
Please help, you could be saving lives . . .

Joanne Perkins (13)
The St Leonards Academy, St Leonards-On-Sea

Love's For Us

Love is red like a rose in summer
It tastes like fresh strawberries and cream
It smells like fresh cut grass on a daisy field
It feels like fluffy clouds floating in the air
It sounds like an angel playing the harp
Is there someone out there for me?
Plenty say there's more fish in the sea!
But love's not easy
Love is sweet
But sometimes it's hard.

Kiera Holly Edwards (12)
The St Leonards Academy, St Leonards-On-Sea

Gymnastics!

Gold, silver, bronze
You might have a chance,
Mum, Dad and family proudly cheering you on,
National qualifiers here I come,
As I stand on the podium I feel very successful,
So proud of yourself and your partners for doing amazing,
Tumbling, preparational, recreational and acro all so great,
In every grade it's so close but there is only one winner,
Counting the score for the final results,
Sweat, blood, tears and chalk are the main features of a gymnast!

Cody Robertson (12)
The St Leonards Academy, St Leonards-On-Sea

Best Friends Are Endless!

We started in school and never ended.
Through tears and fights
Through smiles and giggles
I had always loved you.

Because whenever I needed you
Whenever I was depressed
Like an angel you were there for me.

Every beautiful day we would hang out
And our friendship would still be endless!

Kasia Kader (12)
The St Leonards Academy, St Leonards-On-Sea

Riots

Crack! Glass shatters
Bang! Bombs go off
People smashing into shops
In a flash the police are here to stop the rioting

In an instant the police are stopping the riot
And stopping the people from stealing things
From the shops that were smashed into

Also to stop the riot
And to put an end to all this raging madness.

Calum Howard (14)
The St Leonards Academy, St Leonards-On-Sea

Oh Grapes

Oh grapes
Your smell and your taste are indescribable
You are just as special to me as a close family member
But nothing can compare to you, nothing at all
Your beautiful pale skin is as smooth as a lovely silk shirt
Oh grapes, sweet tasty grapes
You are a meal for kings and a snack for gods
But to me you are perfect
Oh grapes.

David Thomson (14)
The St Leonards Academy, St Leonards-On-Sea

Leave

Please leave me now before your scent is permanently stained on my sheets
Please leave before I know how that scar got on your chest
Please leave before I open up and tell you how the last one loved alcohol more than me
And the one before that tore me open and used my heart to fill someone else's empty space
Please leave me before you trace your fingers over every scar on my body and tell me that
I am beautiful no matter what.

Emily Pascoe-Marchant (14)
The St Leonards Academy, St Leonards-On-Sea

The Planet

I am the sun shining over the world
I am the moon glowing over mountains
I am the stars floating above the Earth
I am the sea waving up to the sand.

Cameron Hill (13)
The St Leonards Academy, St Leonards-On-Sea

My Feelings

I am the sun shining on the world
I am the moon glowing on the Earth
I am the sea crashing against the rocks
I am the stars glistening in the night sky
I am the rain pounding onto the lake
I am the wind blowing through the trees
I am a thunderstorm crashing in the sky
I am a blizzard freezing down your spine
I am the snow icing your heart.

Harmony Evans-Dolan (13)
The St Leonards Academy, St Leonards-On-Sea

So Sad

I am so mad
And a little sad
I don't want to be bad
I am sorry Dad
I am just a bad son
'Why did you do it Ron?'
As I walked home in shame
It won't now be the same
I always wanted fame.

Josh Sissens (13)
The St Leonards Academy, St Leonards-On-Sea

Untitled

The people on the beach were light on their feet
As they swiftly skipped having a big speech
Chuckling cheerfully happy everywhere
Even at the death it will still be brightened up!

Cameron Jones (11)
The St Leonards Academy, St Leonards-On-Sea

Pizza

Oh pizza,
How your steam warms me up
With your lava-like cheese
Melted on your soft, cushion-like crust.
I love the taste of all your toppings,
I love the smell of them too,
Pizza, tasty, lovely pizza
You bring me up when I'm feeling blue.
Pizza, I love you, I do.

Carl Lawrence (13)
The St Leonards Academy, St Leonards-On-Sea

Untitled

Pretty smiles
Deceiving laughs
And people who dream with their eyes open
Lonely cries
And souls who have given up hoping
The other thing that breaks hearts
Are fairy tales that never come true
And selfish people who lie to me
Selfish people just like you.

Perrie O'Connor (14)
The St Leonards Academy, St Leonards-On-Sea

What I Am

I am the sea floating into the clear blue sky
I am the sun shining in the clear blue sky
I am the stars glowing in the night sky
I am the moon lighting up the snow on the mountains.

Daniel Thomas (13)
The St Leonards Academy, St Leonards-On-Sea

Superheroes

I was babysitting a young boy at his house wearing shorts
The young boy called me a superhero
He poked at the marks on my legs and called me a superhero
He told me his daddy was a superhero
He told me his daddy was very strong
The young boy said his daddy tried to fly once
But . . .
The young boy told me . . .
A rope stopped him.

Abi Wood (12)
The St Leonards Academy, St Leonards-On-Sea

Earthquake

Did you hear the breaking news?
An earthquake in Nepal
If we give them money
They can get homes, food and water
Their country has been destroyed
And a lot of people have died
They have lost their loved ones
What will people do to help us?
They ask and ask and ask.

Alfie Morris (12)
The St Leonards Academy, St Leonards-On-Sea

Excitement

Excitement is like joyful flowers blooming
It tastes like magnificent mouth-watering sweets
It looks like colourful butterflies looping
It feels like getting a surprising treat.

Besi Dauti (12)
The St Leonards Academy, St Leonards-On-Sea

One Tragedy In Nepal

One tragedy, a thousand broken families
Have mercy on them, support them
Those who lost who they loved most
Mourn them, respect them.
One tragedy, a million broken families,
Have mercy on them, support them
Those who lost who they loved most
Mourn them, respect them.

Luke Furminger (13)
The St Leonards Academy, St Leonards-On-Sea

You Might Think I'm Crazy

You might think I'm crazy
But there was once a time when I was young
Men used to use rockets to fly to the moon
And bullet jets touched the stars
And felt on top of the world
I know you think I'm a crazy old man
What do I know?
I'm just a crazy old man.

Kai Wright (12)
The St Leonards Academy, St Leonards-On-Sea

Sports

S nowboarding down the mountain of snow
P arasailing across the seven seas
O lympics, achieving your dream goals
R ock climbing up the steep mountain with a sight to remember
T ae kwon do, the masters of throwing people
S occer, shooting for victory against the opposition.

Harry Simmons (12)
The St Leonards Academy, St Leonards-On-Sea

Poetry

Poetry, it's useless
I think it's absolutely pointless
I will never use it
It has no impact on my life
This isn't a poem
It's not poetic
That's the end
Get over it.

Frankie Walsh (14)
The St Leonards Academy, St Leonards-On-Sea

Brighton Pier!

Waiting in line to reach the fluffy candyfloss
The sun reaching the horizon to reveal the pink skies above
The lights start reflecting onto the still waters
Children's laughter could be heard all around
Then the distinct smell of fish 'n' chips reaches my nose
Eventually the moon is put on display to the people all around
The striped deckchairs abandoned
The streets were emptied as the night sky was exposed.

Millie Ancell
The St Leonards Academy, St Leonards-On-Sea

Untitled

Relaxed is blue like the flat sea,
It tastes like bubblegum ice cream
It smells like tropical fruit
It looks like a beautiful view
It sounds like the morning birds chirping
It feels like sunbathing in the sun on holiday.

Emily Couch (12)
The St Leonards Academy, St Leonards-On-Sea

Irate

I am a bull tearing down a corridor
I am a thunder cloud ready to explode
I am a kettle warming up loudly
I am a volcano ready to erupt
I am a witch ready to laugh loudly
I am a door slamming against a wall
I am an angry cloud ready to thunder on people
I am a hasty person pushing people out of the way.

Connor Gray (11)
The St Leonards Academy, St Leonards-On-Sea

Fear

Fear is purple like Halloween Night
The creak of a floor to give you a fright
It smells like sorrow and lots of pain
The boiling of blood inside your vein
It looks like tears dripping off a cheek
Like shadows hidden away in the woods that are bleak
It feels like a shiver travelling down your spine
Believe me when I tell you, it won't be just fine.

Kiera Post (12)
The St Leonards Academy, St Leonards-On-Sea

Love

Love is magenta like loving hearts
Love tastes as sweet as a cherry
Love smells like apple tarts
Love looks as delightful as a berry
Love sounds like calming voices
Love feels like a bunch of choices.

Bethany McDonald (12)
The St Leonards Academy, St Leonards-On-Sea

Hatred Throughout The World

Filled with rage as I walk down the street
Fighting for the little guy in my life
When I'm filled with rage, fury and horror
I always strive to feel that goodness
Will never come as long as I'm in time.
I know I'm doing the right thing at the right time
There are more people that will never see the light of day
The world hates us all.

William Scott (12)
The St Leonards Academy, St Leonards-On-Sea

Happiness

Happiness is yellow just like the sun
It tastes like your favourite food out in the sun
It's like having fun in the sun
Fun is smiles, not like an annoying boy
Having laughter in the sun
Happiness is like being a ball bounced around
Cheerfulness is the sun
Happiness is always in the sun.

Chloe Sarah Anne Paterson (13)
The St Leonards Academy, St Leonards-On-Sea

What Is Love?

You are as beautiful as a rose
A soft touch in every pose
When you are in a small and soulless sadness
I will always be there with a happy smile
It makes me feel so soft
To always see your face again.

Dylan Love (13)
The St Leonards Academy, St Leonards-On-Sea

Oh Chocolate!

Oh chocolate you are so delicious
You are creamy and sweet
As sweet as a freshly made cupcake
I love your taste and texture
As you just melt in the mouth
If you weren't in my life
Oh chocolate
Nothing would be the same!

Sophia Saxby (12)
The St Leonards Academy, St Leonards-On-Sea

Untitled

Filled with sadness I look at my house and look at theirs
They're so sad and I feel bad
They're poor and have nothing to sit on
Except the floor.
Here I am, look at them lying on the floor
Death, death, death, they have no grave
And I have to wave goodbye
And they lie down and die.

Alfie Smith (13)
The St Leonards Academy, St Leonards-On-Sea

Apocalypse!

A, B, C, D, E, F, G gummy bears are chasing me
One is red, one is blue, one is peeing on my shoe
Now the red one has a knee and I'm running for my life
Two days later I met an alligator
He said he would eat me later
And that I looked yummy like a gummy bear.

Derrin Moss (11)
The St Leonards Academy, St Leonards-On-Sea

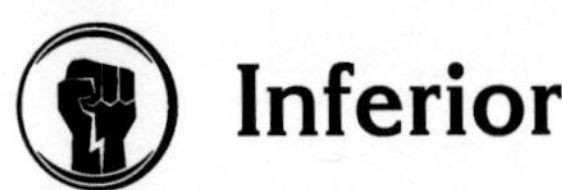

Inferior

I inhale, the resentment growing ever stronger
The antagonism between us so strong they can hide it no longer
They're the puppet masters, we're their puppets, they pull the strings
They take our freedom, along with other things
A life beyond this is my only dream
If we work as a team we can come up with a scheme
To break their hold
And leave their hearts of cold.

Jessica Coker (13)
The St Leonards Academy, St Leonards-On-Sea

VE Day

Cheers surround the air, people jump up and down
A car is driving around as Winston Churchill comes to town.

A special message is going to be sent,
Winston Churchill came up to the balcony and says:
'Victory is ours, Britain has won!' Everyone cheers and up the confetti goes.

1945 was the year, the year the war ended,
Everything was over, families were so happy that everything was mended.

Carl Hitchman
The St Leonards Academy, St Leonards-On-Sea

I Can't Write Poems

I can't write poems
It's really annoying
I'm not poetic
I was unpoemed at birth
I want to go home
I can't write poems.

Millie Garing (14)
The St Leonards Academy, St Leonards-On-Sea

Spain

I always love going on holiday to Spain
The scorching sun burning my skin
The soft breezy wind, blows through my hair

Late night walks across the golden sand
The waves of the clear blue sea
The view of the beautiful sunset in the distance
Shining on the clear bright blue sea.

Holli Jessica Ferguson (12)
The St Leonards Academy, St Leonards-On-Sea

Animals

A nimals are creatures which we shall love
N o one should hurt them
I will care for all animals
M an should not kill for sport
A lso for fun
L ove all animals around
S hare what you have with animals.

Robert Poulter (14)
The St Leonards Academy, St Leonards-On-Sea

Human Life

L ife is a roller coaster flying by
I t can make people happy, sometimes sad, people suffering in poor conditions
F ighting is a problem, many people die; rich countries, poor countries, not many people survive
E ventually things get better, that's not a lie, but people cope, save each other and fight to survive.

Leah Williams (12)
The St Leonards Academy, St Leonards-On-Sea

Happiness

Happy is orange like a sunny day
It tastes like pizza
It smells like sugar and sweets
It looks like a lovely rainbow and a golden beach
It sounds like birds tweeting
It feels amazing
It makes you smile.

Kaden Dunford (13)
The St Leonards Academy, St Leonards-On-Sea

Ode To Happiness

Ode to happiness, it is blue like a clear sky
It is the taste of melted ice cream
Dripping sensationally down the cone
It is like the fresh season of spring
It is like the looks of a cheerful and crowded street
It is like the cheers of people
It is the feeling of the best start.

Daisy Mai Hilton (12)
The St Leonards Academy, St Leonards-On-Sea

I Am Relaxed

I am relaxed like a light blue sky
It tastes like a shortbread biscuit
It smells buttery and sweet
It looks like a pretty flower blossoming
It feels like an ice pole melting in the sun
It sounds like a soft, satisfying crunch
I am relaxed.

Scarlett Prentice (12)
The St Leonards Academy, St Leonards-On-Sea

Rising Sun

The sun shines very kind over the gracious clouds
The people lay on grass head to feet and life can pass on by
The hearts of the people store patriotism galore
And their history's no bore when you see them at the core
Of festivals and parties with much more
Their architecture is more than pretty looks and can't be mistook
As just stories in books about great points in the country's history.

Arron Hales (14)
The St Leonards Academy, St Leonards-On-Sea

Football Mad!

A man tripped me over and I roared at him
Fire was going through my eyes
His name was Tim
He was full of lies
I glared devilishly at him
We came face-to-face
He looked at me with the eye of death in the middle of my face!

Jack Davis (11)
The St Leonards Academy, St Leonards-On-Sea

Untitled

Happiness is like blue sunny days
It tastes like ice cream
It smells like freshly picked bananas
It looks like a shiny beach ball of happiness
Bouncing through the sky
I am a smile taking in the memories
I am a human.

Tazzie Way (12)
The St Leonards Academy, St Leonards-On-Sea

Untitled

Living with anxiety it's like being followed by a voice
It knows your insecurities and uses them against you.
It gets to the point where it's the loudest voice in the room
The only one you can hear
And points out all your faults
The worst part is, the voice is probably lying
But you can't stop listening.

Sophie Britt (12)
The St Leonards Academy, St Leonards-On-Sea

Forever

Forever we stand here, blind to the future
Lost to our past and enduring our torture
Forever we take chances to settle our battles
Losing some fights and winning some fights
Forever we pray out loud, hoping someone will hear
Forever crying softly but never shedding a tear
Forever we stand here fighting for our freedom.

JC Collins (13)
The St Leonards Academy, St Leonards-On-Sea

Love

I love that place
I love that band
1D
And most of all
I love food
I love that smile
My friends give me.

Hannah Rose Morris (12)
The St Leonards Academy, St Leonards-On-Sea

My Best Friend

He's my little piece of perfection
But he doesn't believe it
So he picks up the blade, turns up the music and zones out from the world
He's hurting
He doesn't realise he's hurting me too
Cuts on his wrists, his stomach and thighs
Are like a million on mine.

Lauren Smth (14)
The St Leonards Academy, St Leonards-On-Sea

Untitled

The door slams
When my sky turns grey
Everything freezes when it happens
When it happens
I see red
And you see
Nothing.

Spike Grimshaw Harris (12)
The St Leonards Academy, St Leonards-On-Sea

Bacon . . .

Oh sweet bacon
How you grab my attention at an instant
Oh delicious bacon
You are my everlasting love
Oh glorious bacon
May your majesticness live on through the years
You, bacon, are the one and only thing I would have at any time.

Callum Moss (12)
The St Leonards Academy, St Leonards-On-Sea

Home

Oh! My favourite place
I love that place called home
My home is a happy place
I love my home
I want to tell the world
How amazing my home is
I love my home!

Oliver Wray (12)
The St Leonards Academy, St Leonards-On-Sea

Sports

Soccer kicking a ball across the grass
Paragliding off the mountains.
Parachuting out of a plane
Climbing up Mount Everest
Canoeing across The Channel
Cycling through the streets of London
Running up the Great Wall of China.

Alfie Ridley (11)
The St Leonards Academy, St Leonards-On-Sea

The General Election

The great election has been a bit of an infection
People want a cure
Doctors say there is not an injection for this major infection
But people are unsure
Party leaders fell one by one
Leaving the outdone David Cameron ready to rule the country.

Bradley James Patrick O'Toole (12)
The St Leonards Academy, St Leonards-On-Sea

Friends

I love my friends
Funny and sad
Good times and bad
I want to tell the world
How amazing they are
I love my friends.

Keiron Addams (12)
The St Leonards Academy, St Leonards-On-Sea

Me

I am a blizzard blustering through your bones
I am a thunderstorm pounding against the sky
I am the snow freezing your rooftops
I am the rain dripping on the lake
I am the wind howling down your chimney.

Reece Lavender (13)
The St Leonards Academy, St Leonards-On-Sea

Happiness

I am a fiery ball of happiness
I am a rosy red rose
I am a sweet smell of chocolate melting
I am the taste of a rippled raspberry
Does this make you happy?

Ivy Potter (12)
The St Leonards Academy, St Leonards-On-Sea

I Am The Weather

I am a thunderstorm, crashing through the sky
I am the rain sprinkling stars on the lake
I am the wind howling past your window
I am a blizzard, freezing your bones
I am the snow, icing your heart.

Rosie Hoare (14)
The St Leonards Academy, St Leonards-On-Sea

What I Do In Hastings

Hastings is beautiful as can be
The mountains are amazing and so is the sea
But what I like to do in Hastings
Is be with my friends and family
And always be there for them.

Lewis Dunn
The St Leonards Academy, St Leonards-On-Sea

Untitled

Happy is the colour of a beautiful rainbow shining brightly
It tastes like strawberry laces completely covered in sugar
It smells like flowers fully born on a sunny day
It sounds like birds singing their delightful songs
It feels like home, warm and cosy.

Lee Keeley (13)
The St Leonards Academy, St Leonards-On-Sea

Untitled

Happiness, luminous yellow like the sun
It tastes like mountains of sweets
Happiness looks like a banana smiling
Happiness is excitement inside you
It sounds like birds tweeting in the summer.

Wade Thunder (12)
The St Leonards Academy, St Leonards-On-Sea

Untitled

Sadness fills the room
The tears run down my face
You made me feel this way
Things will never be the same
Without you I am lost.

Courtney Amber Beeching (13)
The St Leonards Academy, St Leonards-On-Sea

Winter

I am a thunderstorm crashing through the door
Looking to seek and revenge
I am the snow smothering the rooftops like ice cream
I am a blizzard blustering through your hair like a knife
I am the wind whistling past your feet ready to trip you.

Callum Fox (14)
The St Leonards Academy, St Leonards-On-Sea

Have You Felt . . .

Have you felt like lava soaring through your veins?
Imagine you're a tear of blood,
Creating aversion where there should be none
Screams of fear ring, ring through your ears
No one, no one knows how it feels to fear
Being a teenager, it's hard,
You have to be the best or you're the worst
Downgraded from the others
Sometimes I feel like a fear
A zombie or vampire
That fear light and love
People fear and don't hear me
No one knows how it feels to be me
Imagine that just once
Then maybe everything will change
Just once.

Tyler Lee Newlands (13)
The St Leonards Academy, St Leonards-On-Sea

YOUNG WRITERS INFORMATION

We hope you have enjoyed reading this book – and that you will continue to in the coming years.

If you're a young writer who enjoys reading and creative writing, or the parent of an enthusiastic poet or story writer, do visit our website **www.youngwriters.co.uk**. Here you will find free competitions, workshops and games, as well as recommended reads, a poetry glossary and our blog.

If you would like to order further copies of this book, or any of our other titles, give us a call or visit **www.youngwriters.co.uk.**

Young Writers,
Remus House
Coltsfoot Drive,
Peterborough,
PE2 9BF

(01733) 890066 / 898110
info@youngwriters.co.uk